OK GEN Z

THE TRUE GENERATION

NEERJA SINGH

Notion Press Media Pvt Ltd

No. 50, Chettiyar Agaram Main Road,
Vanagaram, Chennai, Tamil Nadu – 600 095

First Published by Notion Press 2021
Copyright © Neerja Singh 2021
All Rights Reserved.

ISBN 978-1-68509-628-1

Dedication

To Col and Mrs H S Sangha (Retd)
and the life and lessons they are giving their grandchildren Aqseer,
Asawari, Ajrawar, Nirbhay, Nirmolika, Niyamat and Chitralekha

Contents

Foreword — 7

Acknowledgement — 9

Preface — 11

1. Touchy Feely — 13
2. Power of Appreciation — 17
3. Screen Time Panic — 21
4. New Age Parents — 25
5. The Whipping Boy — 29
6. Zoomer's Teacher — 33
7. Come Back Hobbies — 38
8. Death from Work — 42
9. Public Display of Affection — 46
10. Millennial's Envy — 50
11. High School Dating — 54
12. To Snap or No — 58
13. Gen Z's Watershed Moment — 62
14. The Snake People — 66
15. OK Gen Z — 70
16. Industry of Guilt — 74
17. The Amazeballs — 78
18. The Matchmaker — 82

19. Here They Come 86

20. The Moral Code 91

21. As Good as Our Stories 95

22. The Koreaboos 99

23. The Critical Prevention 103

24. The Covid Feminism 107

25. Mothers Across the Generations 111

26. The New Dad 115

27. The Vaping Point 119

28. The Mighty Parent 123

29. The Anxious Inheritors 127

30. The Kinder Shopper 131

Foreword

I frequently interact with my grandparents. They share narratives about the world during the 40s, 50s, and 60s. My parents share perspectives on pre and post-liberalisation, pre & post-privatisation and pre & post-globalisation.

I understand one thing. The world is going through a tremendous shift in consciousness. The citizens who awaken to this consciousness are labeled as Gen Z.

I wrote the book 'My Unskooled Year' at the age of 15. This book recounts my experiences on taking a sabbatical from school after my 10th. This one year gave me an insight into how the economic engine works. I understood it through my experiences in the stock market and internships in a dozen industries. WE ARE GOING TOWARDS A BRICK-LESS, MOTOR-LESS, CRYPTO WORLD AND GEN Z IS FUELLING THIS CAUSE AND ADDING MOMENTUM TO IT.

As the world gets digitalized, I see that structure of the middlemen crumbling. I see a world of financial advisors, auditors, wholesalers, mandis, insurance agents becoming nonexistent. The Millennials with the rapid spread of digitization are fast catapulting us into a new world.

I am a prime example of schools being an institution of the past that have a minimal role in the future. Covid is furthering this cause. With this providing customised education, schools of the industrial era will cease to exist.

Author Neerja Singh is a woman I admire. A strong woman who has stood the test of time, she has a smiling demeanor and a soft heart. A person who is always on a quest to know more and a bridge between the then and the now (Gen Z). She has always given me suggestions, nudged me, and has been a constant source of energy. Gen Z needs it when we wade through tumultuous waters.

I would urge the readers to also read the book 'Zero to One' by Peter Thiel. In the very last chapter, he posts scenarios; one of doomsday, one of the worlds going through cycles, and one of the worlds growing exponentially into a different stratosphere. This is the world we perceive. A world of no governance, a world of collaborativeness, a world of transparency, and a world of love.

I am a dreamer and I'm not the only one. Neerja Ma'am leads this tribe of dreamers. She is marching them towards a visionary world, a Xanadu, a utopian world, and the garden of Eden.

N. R. Narayana Murthy, founder of Infosys once said, "I paint a rainbow and each member of my team puts a piece into his pocket". Author Neerja has painted a rainbow, put a piece of it in your pocket.

Sagarikka Sivakumar

Growth Ignitor | Investor |
Teenage Author of 'My Unskooled Year' | Speaker |
Documentary - Eat Fast Die Young | Gen Z

https://www.sagarikka.com/

Acknowledgement

This book is an outcome of a 30 days blogging challenge held by the Professional Speakers Association of India, one of the seventeen worldwide speaker associations affiliated to the Global Speakers Federation. The initiative was led by Dr Latha Vijaybaskar, Leadership Coach and Author https://drlathavijaybaskar.com/.

Preface

Consumption was the expression of ideology for the Baby Boomers, born 1940 to 1959.

Status was what Gen Xers, born 1960-79, consumed.

Millennials, born 1980–94, sought and consumed experiences.

For Generation Z, consumption is driven by the search for truth, in their personal identities as well as their world view. Memories of the Covid-19 seared into their collective consciousness, they will, for the rest of their lives carry that moment when their world came to a grinding halt. Fuelled by a vision of their uncertain future, consumption means access to them rather than possession, consumption is as an expression of individual identity, and it is a matter of ethical concern.

The four core Gen Z behaviors are all anchored in their search for truth. Individual expression matters more than labels. This Clicktivist generation will mobilize themselves for a range of causes. They would rather use dialogues for conflict resolutions. Their decisions and relationship with institutions are based on pragmatic analysis.

They truly are the "True Gen."

Leave them to be themselves, they feel freer with the internet. Don't use stereotypes on them. Their identities take time to shape. They are not asking for permission to be identity nomads, they simply are. Not for them the heaviness of charades. Not for them the games of public-facing social platforms. It is over tighter online destinations, the "digital campfires" that they connect and shape the culture around them.

The TikTok generation is forever evaluating humongous amounts of information and influences, and it is on the self that it experiments, tests and brings about changes first. They are far more serious about defending human rights than the earlier generations. Inclusive in a radical way, they don't tell online friends from the offline. Unlike the cohorts gone before, Gen Z is able to interact through their differences with the system including their families.

This generation of self-learners is not as rosy eyed as the Millennials. They know they will need to save the future. Gig economy, collaborative work, multiple sources of income, their consumption in particular is anchored in ethics. Commitment to environmental, social and governance issues matter to them; equality and climate change being causes they align with.

Gen Z is growing up through a trial by fire. They bring to the real world greater empathy and adaptability, having expereinced disruption in their own lives. Their emotional intelligence comes from losing friends and family to the virus.

There is a flip side however. The Zoomers also present acute loneliness, anxiety and depression. That makes a strong case for intergenerational empathy and generational fluency.

Neerja Singh

Touchy Feely

It is world events that shape generations and we still do not know for certain what exactly will be the long-term fallout of Covid-19 on school children who were suddenly confined to their homes. We may not know for many years the related data and analysis. But collectively, this startling change in the way they lived counts for a large-scale human trauma. These formative experiences are certain to shape their views of the world. This generation will evolve certain characteristics that we do not yet know.

Under the circumstances, what can parents and teachers do to help them prepare for the uncertainty ahead? What are the potential areas where research and reorientation and redesigning will be needed to ease their eventual entry into the new real world?

Take skill development. For the past few months, the options that have been exercised by schools and educational institutions are bound to have long term consequences. Gen Z's (born between 1996 to 2015) training schedule has been disrupted in multiple ways. In most cases, the curriculum had to be quickly converted to online formats by amateurs in this field. Direct instructions were discarded and students and parents worked on independent projects, bolstered by digital resources. Learning struggled to happen at home amidst families and pets in spaces that call for a particular preparation. In many a case, grades were abandoned in favour of pass or fail status. Tests became a casualty and deadlines rubber bands, stretching away merrily.

What has this loss of structure done to the children? Has it disoriented them, causing confusion and conflict? Does it mean that the adults will need to exercise greater patience and be prepared to mentor and support in stronger ways? Have reorientation programs been conceived to ease their transition back to regular school when that happens? A comprehensive return would ideally involve rethinking the usual focus on academics, offering instead mentorship in making sense of their most recent experiences.

Remote learning arrangements may endure in the form of modified timetables. There have been changes in age and gender demographics. Technological improvements and the global nature of human engagement had begun to shout flexibility even before the Covid-19 struck. This culture of fluidity is sure to demand new shifts and learning opportunities. Inter-generational relationships will need to be stronger than ever before; teachers will stand to benefit from being open to reverse mentoring, schools will need to devote time and resources to building a stronger multi-generational culture.

The second area that continues to create a buzz is stress management. The baseline for school students today is already higher than the generations before and research is clear that childhood exposure to sustained stress will impact mental and social development. Have schools put into place empathetic plans to assist the students with their mental health struggles? The most effective stress management program is one that functions at multiple levels, home, class room and organizational. And of these, the most sustainable results are likely to come from organizational policies.

When the class room reopens, the young lives will resume with some form of anxiety and ambivalence. Open conversations, supportive environments, pro-active interventions will likely keep the odd minor challenge from becoming a life crisis. It will be important to remind oneself constantly of the large-scale interruption the young have experienced in all that motivated and fulfilled them earlier. The stake holders involved will also need greater stocks of emotional intelligence than pre-pandemic. And we can no longer afford to await this skill some more years down the road ahead. The future we are looking at now will not have as much use for hard training as it will for an emotional equipment. Tomorrow's workforce, the educators, professionals and innovators will need psychological robustness and wholesomeness most of all.

What is the current rate of psychopathology of the Indian teens? Do we know? Teens for instance, in the United States exhibit stress edging past that of adults. It is believed that their rate of psychopathology is five times that of 75 years ago. Lowered school achievement, unwanted pregnancy, binge drinking, use of marijuana, school violence, obesity, foggy misery, STDs…there is an overwhelming anxiety and at times acute depression during the school years. Could these be symptomatic of a complete lack of investment in the training of children's "non-cognitive" skills? Do our young have the motivation, the ability to persevere and the degree of self-control that is needed to take the economy and well-being of the race forward?

Feelings matter at home and at work. Emotion science, positive psychology and mindfulness curriculums have begun to address the management of feelings. It is also called the art of managing one's micro-expressions, the frown and the smile! The ability to analyse and selectively choose emotions is related to happier outcomes in children as early as pre-school. The real benefits include deeper friendships, stronger attachments with teachers and parents, smarter conflict management, sharper academic scores and non-threatening leadership skills.

There is growing evidence by now to establish that Social Emotional Learning (SEL) programs are effective and sorely needed in schools. The policies and funds needed however are crushingly slow in coming. How then do we begin to fund the teachers' SEL training.? There are agencies out there that offer evidence based SEL programming that should make support for the education of emotions easier. Nothing less than an emotional revolution is the need of the hour today. We are already a quarter way into the new century.

Has there been any dialogue in schools with the students? Do we know how they feel in the school, how different is it from what they would like to feel and what can be done to bridge the gap? It ought to be done anonymously if needed but there is a pressing case to get them to share ideas with business leaders, educators, policymakers so that the learning environments can be upgraded with a sense of urgency.

Social and emotional skills are not 'soft' but the 'hardest' we will need beginning now. A compassionate vigilance, keener empathy and a resilient adaptability will be the features of the next generation of leaders. This generation has been tested young and deserves all the support to herald the evolution of the human race they look destined to lead, God help them.

Power of Appreciation

We had Miss Flower teach us English at the St Francis Convent High School, Jhansi. She would send me out on an errand so she could read my essays out to the class without fear of giving me a big head. Praise was not as forthcoming as it is today with the new generations.

Why, it is not unusual for Gen Z to demand and expect appreciation. It is also quite acceptable for them to declare dissatisfaction at work for instance and seek better experiences elsewhere. An unusually large percentage of Generation Z are sitting on the fence at their places of work at any given time.

This generation is different. Words of appreciation are not enough. It is financial recognition, even in micro ways that gives them a greater sense of personal fulfilment and loyalty to their employer. Appreciation for their work and rewards given in the right way have the power to turn them into enthusiastic and valuable resources for their organization.

Gen Z responds to shared identity, a sense of belonging, social rewards and progress feedback. They look for peer-to-peer interaction, engagement and sharing. And this sentiment is seeping into our social and professional spaces, via osmosis. And justifiably so.

If we were to sit down and put pen to paper or fingertips to the keyboard, what is that one sentiment we are hungry for under our controlled masks? The feeling of being valued! That belief that we are in some way unique. A reassurance that we have something truly special to offer the world. This validation from the environment is the thrust that will keep us orbiting with the occasional lift offs. It is the battery cable to our self-esteem. The ointment to our hidden sores.

And the word is 'appreciation'.

What if we were to replicate this exchange consciously? What if we could each give the other this natural shot of mood lifter? What if we could dance through life knowing that we are seen? What if this crying need to be seen and heard was met at regular intervals?

The impact appreciation has on us gets buried under the debris of the daily humdrum. We get so busy racing after goals and projects and mental pictures of where we are headed, we let the present slip through our fingers. Appreciation is powerful. It can craft our relationships and affect how we see ourselves. It is pretty much known that the number one reason employees leave their place of work is because they do not feel valued by their environment. It is an ethereal thing; appreciation is felt only when people pour themselves into each other. Mike Robbins, the author of "Focus on the Good Stuff" espouses that it is not about recognizing results and performance. Recognition is limited and based on performance whereas appreciation is about recognizing the value of people.

Appreciation is when you make a conscious choice to acknowledge something or someone. It happens when we tell ourselves, "Hold on, here is something powerful. There is breath, there is this being, there is beauty in our common struggle to just be with dignity and grace. I appreciate this." Researchers claim that there is increased activity in key areas of the "appreciative brains" that light up and are correlated to emotional processing and interpersonal bonding. Appreciation is known to improve cognitive abilities and a general sense of well-being.

A study by Glassdoor found that 81% of employees surveyed felt motivated to work harder when their boss showed appreciation. Even with increased productivity, the stunning fact is that appreciation in the workplace lags far behind expressions of appreciation in society at large. So, there we have it, we are less likely to give or receive appreciation in our workplaces — where we spend the majority of our waking hours — than anywhere else in our lives. Even more disheartening is that a whopping majority admits to rarely ever expressing gratitude at work.

We have got to change this since expressing appreciation is a proven positive force. No matter where we are in the scheme and hierarchy of things, acknowledging each other above, across or below helps everybody feel appreciated, valued and rewarded. And the gratitude spill over effect is enormous: the domino effect of appreciation causes people who experience gratitude to feel happier and spread that happiness, increasing trust and collaboration among colleagues.

Is it all just about a simple "thank you"? Well, yes and no. Yes, thanking others is the next right thing, but mechanically voiced platitudes can fall flat, seem insincere, and backfire. The best way to cultivate gratitude is to be appreciative, in other words be intentional, thoughtful, and authentic while acknowledging another human being. One does not even have to like another or be the best of friends with them in order to do that. All one is doing is checking in with another on how they are doing and not just what they are doing.

There is such a din around us about positivity and mindfulness, one wonders when it is going to hit the point of saturation and fade away only to be replaced by new catch phrases. Truth be told, the normative values have remained unchanged since antiquity, it is just our comprehension and acceptance and internalizing of these that changes with the vocabulary of our times. The "do unto your neighbour" biblical call is "social reciprocity" today, for instance.

To be seen, to be acknowledged, to be accepted is a fundamental need with each one of us. Who has not used these phrases with conviction, "I believe" or "I am convinced" or "In my experience" or "I will have you know"? These voices come from a deeply felt spiritual need for self-definition, self-affirmation, self-authentication. Who are you? Where are you going? What more could you be doing? These are the questions that drive us to live, they decide our one-moment-to-another choices and actions. So then, did your day go well? Or was it spent just reacting?

The exemplary thing to do would be to begin by receiving compliments in a gracious manner. Many a times, there is a tendency to negate the appreciation by contesting it, dismissing it or just plain explaining it. A gracious acceptance would establish self-value and model appreciation right away. It would also alleviate somewhat the disquiet we're experiencing inside our socially-distanced bubbles.

Screen Time Panic

There is a moral panic about screen time today. Is it good or bad? What kind of screen time is positive and what may be detrimental? Is it right for certain states in India to ban online learning? How much screen time is recommended? What are the best practices and safeguards necessary for maintaining the physical and mental well-being of kids during the virtual mode of learning?

Every generation faces disruptive technologies, yet why does today's version seem like the end of civilization? It is not as though humans have not panicked before. Enlightenment, literacy, the industrial revolution all brought fear and uncertainty to us but we shifted gears, metamorphosed and moved on.

Jean Twenge, psychology professor at San Diego State University and author of the book *iGen,* says this time is different because it's "much more sudden and pronounced" than previous generational shifts. Tristan Harris, former design ethicist at Google opines that "this is about the war for attention and where that's taking society." The image being evoked is that of "a thousand engineers" on the other side of the screen, working on "persuasive design" to snare our young.

It is true that more valuable memories can be created by spending time with friends and families. It is also feared that teens begin to lose the socializing skill with too much screen time. And then, there is the Computer Vision Syndrome involving dry eyes, blurry vision, soreness and light sensitivity. Alternately there are action video games that are considered good for hand eye coordination. There is enough and more out there about harm reduction. Sit about 20 to 26 inches away from the screen, it has been recommended. Dim the overhead light to reduce the glare. Get some sunshine and exercise. Take frequent breaks. But how about the Gen Z (born 1995 to 2015) many of whom feel their more authentic selves online?

The story of human civilization has followed a linear path. A truth surfaces then science takes a while to catch up with it and the rest then fetch up having debated and made peace with the new truth. And this newness is closer than we think it is. Google's Expedition App, an immersive teaching and learning tool is already here, harbinger of the virtual reality lessons. There is a picture of the near future emerging matrix like, bolstered with augmented reality, complete with 3D printed houses and robots for house companions. Delivery by drones, hyper loops for inter-city transportation, advanced prosthetic such as an arm with a built in flashlight, cybernetic implants for leg strength, exoskeleton suits that will make the wearer stronger, faster, taller, Spiderman suits, polymer gel leggings…mankind is inching up towards computer consciousness, the deep mind. There is no getting away from screens, in other words.

It is only the policy makers that stand between Cyborgs becoming a reality in just twenty five more years. We are currently living in a connected world; the spirit of information networks shapes our everyday experiences. The metaphor for our consciousness is the language of digital technology. Do we not say "hardwired" for empathetic connection? Why then are we conflicted about letting our kids move into the reality that we have already collectively fashioned. We want to be the gatekeepers to their progress. We forget Kahlil Gibran on children: *For their souls dwell in the house of tomorrow, which you cannot visit, not even in your dreams. The future belongs to them.*

Has childhood ever existed in a vacuum? There has never been a one size fits all, neutral version of the perfect developmental experience. The new generation grows up in context. It plays in ways that will count as preparation to participate in economies. Their mandate is to live productive and fulfilled lives within specific cultural norms. The onus on them is to construct their identity narratives using the tools of the time. The classic wooden toys for instance, grew out of Friedrich Fröbel's 19th century kindergarten movement. The board games and stuffed animals were products of the Industrial Age. I grew up on the spinning top and clay dolls with nodding heads! These objects taught kids to see themselves in ways that aligned with the spirit of a particular time and place.

The question to ask the experts is, "What is the evidence against screens precisely?" Gaya Dowling, a researcher at the National Institutes of Health, USA used MRI brain scans to conclude that kids who engage in digital play for more than seven hours a day have thinning cortexes. This revelation was followed up with an ambivalent rider, "That's typically thought to be a maturational process, so what we would expect to see later is happening a bit earlier." That's really the crux of the problem. Are the researches really studying the kids or just the demographic statistics? Data has come to be used to manage behavioural outcomes. But kids are not just data points; their well-being would involve a more philosophical approach.

What is happening today is being likened to a "natural kind of uncontrolled experiment on the next generation". There simply is not enough data to support any conclusion or warrant the fear mongering going on around us. And what there is of it is being subjected to the new principle of "statistics actually can change what you see." The quality of the science used to determine whether or not screen time is good, the large data sets and statistical methods employed, the ethics of data sharing by researchers looking into the question may have allowed for anomalies to be claimed as significant conclusions.

As a matter of fact, smoking marijuana and being bullied were more closely linked with decreased well-being than tech use was; at the same time, getting enough sleep and regularly eating breakfast were more closely tied to positive feelings than screen time was to negative ones. Let's hasten to clarify though that not finding a strong association doesn't mean that screen time is healthy or safe for young people. Perhaps the risks are being balanced by huge rewards. A screen-related activity may be beneficial or harmful depending on who is doing it, how much they're doing it, when they're doing it and what they're not doing instead.

Ask the kids, 'What are you doing on the screen? What makes you feel good? What makes you feel bad?' We may well find that the slightly negative effect of technology use isn't as bad as say, having a single parent or needing to wear glasses. It is not our jobs as parents and teachers and concerned adults to protect them from an uncertain future. What we can do is to teach them how to apply the old human values — kindness, compassion, ethics, and etiquette — within the new technological contexts.

If the devil is in our smartphones, we needn't worry; the instrument is projected to become extinct in 2025. The answer to the question therefore, of whether screen time is bad for kids is "It depends." And that means figuring out "On what?"

New Age Parents

Parenting is not for the faint-hearted. And parenting in these times of expert advice, judgments, and gentle nudging is nerve-wracking. There is so much confusion and anxiety over all the parenting permutations and combinations available, akin to a collective panic.

What's your template of choice for a child for instance? A science-minded kid? An eco-friendly child? A disease-proof offspring? Or a financially savvy child?

There are recipes for each of those.

There was a time when children were economic assets. They worked and contributed to the family income. It was a reciprocal arrangement. Then along came the concepts of "a child's right" and schools. Children stopped working, the school became work and the load shifted to the parents. And it kept growing in radius because now there was the child's happiness and self-esteem that began to be held up as the absolute moral values. Everyone forgot that these two elusive and ephemeral notions are tied up with effort and pushing and doing things one does not want to do. For the earlier generations, the parents provided this discipline and structure and hateful nagging but for this generation, there was no one after school/college. Not for want of trying but the young themselves developed a very private, independent, and individual sense of self. The personal choice became a virtue and failure began to be celebrated. More confusion. About this time they began to ring true, the words of sociologist Viviana

Zelizer, that children have become "economically worthless but emotionally priceless."

More the cocktail of clashing values, more the furious improvising by the parents. By now they have no clue as to what kind of a future they need to prepare their kids for. It's all changing too fast. So what do the half eager, half scared parents do? They typically try to prepare their children for every eventuality. In other words, the child must have cognitive skills, problem-solving smarts, kinaesthetic talents, and so on, plenty of structured activities. And let's face it, school is never enough. And then there are the experts!

First, they strip the parents of their authority by eulogizing democracy at home. There are no clear guidelines on what the boundaries are supposed to be. In the absence of any script, the parents lurch from being enablers to supporters. Does a child get to choose her school, for instance? At what age? Second, all this frantic parenting is happening in cultures, most of which do not offer basic infrastructure, let alone any state support for child-rearing. It is solely a mother/father team's mandate to equip their child with sustainable skills for survival. Of course, they will do all it takes to ensure their kids have a decent shot at a life of 'enough and dignity'. Today, a typical middle-class family pours everything it has into bringing up the children.

Now presuming that a child does make it to a good school and parents step back with an inherent trust in the highly reputed institution, what then typically follows? Guess what, at the end of five years, they may end up meeting a chaotic stranger shaped by peer parenting and administrative alienation. In many of the educated, aware, progressive families today, parents are getting lectures on 'respecting their space' from adult offspring whose total nurturing experience consists of two low maintenance cats.

These are also the same 'dreams deprived' bunches who espouse the cause of autonomy sitting in their parental homes.

And when they do get on with their dreams, the real world kicks in and the fun begins. There is loneliness, parents are understandably not overly enthused, and they are fatigued a bit with the workings of their child's colonized mind. There are stresses involved; the money takes a long time coming. There is disillusionment because even a dream involves some amount of drudgery. All those TED talks, high school Insta-influencers, and YouTube celebrities come crashing at the young, fuelling their self-doubt and leaving them feeling like oddballs, neither here nor there. Dreams should ideally be chased by young people on their own time and money. A parent's responsibility is to give them an education adequate for financial self-sufficiency.

Why is what was good enough for me, not good enough for my kids? These are constantly evolving new roles parents have to grow into. You are a friend, a sounding board, a mentor, a cheerleader, a role model, just the right balance of softness and toughness. Too much is expected of parents these days. And let's not forget that in the brave new world, the gender roles are changing too. Dads get to be as soft as mums and Mums get to be as tough as dads. There is a recipe for domestic strife! Fathers are known to report greater work/life conflict today.

A handful of our dreamers do succeed, yes. The rest either return home, lesser or diminished…they make a great market for the motivational and setback leadership industry… or they go the Sushant Singh Rajput way. No one but a young person's family is truly invested in her. It is her primary support system. Unfortunately, that loving buffer is under attack and demonization today. Parents are soft targets. They are too petrified of their kids having to suffer so they listen and nod their heads at this talk of "parents living their dreams through their kids". It's as big a lie as the unquestioned dictum today of "happiness and self-esteem". Sure, the parents consider the happiness of their children paramount and they indeed take on custodianship of their self-esteem but we forget that these are not values in themselves. There is no curriculum for happiness and confidence. They cannot be goals unto themselves; this is too big a burden. These are by-products of a work-ethic and productivity.

That's all I did. I tried to teach them decency, morality, and integrity of effort. And I tried very hard not to hurt them. I failed at times. There was a struggle to be self-fulfilled and sacrificing at the same time.

Is all of this called living my dreams through my kids?

The Whipping Boy

This one has always been the whipping boy of TV anchors and panellists. But now the middle class in India is very angry with the middle class only.

It was the Anna phenomenon that threw the Indian middle class into the limelight. For the first time since 1947, a swathe of humanity lifted itself up and marched into the Ramlila grounds and the waiting TV cameras. Until that moment, the lot had remained invisible; they did not vote, they did not agitate, they did not terrorize, they did not steal, they went about their business quietly and stayed off the national radar.

The one thing that fuelled and jettisoned them was the phenomenon of liberalization. While visible India was busy looting the exchequer and wheeling and dealing and living it up, the middle class was adding to its investments in real estate, their children's education, savings plans, and personal entrepreneurship. The prospect of a disposable income, a comfortable lifestyle and future security were factors driving this relentlessly working mass of humanity. Through all this life of drudgery and thrift, their glue and anchor remained the family unit. Needless to say, one generation's drive prompted a saga of growth and opportunity and evolution for the successive progeny.

Along came the pandemic. The carefully balanced structure began to collapse like a house of cards. There is confusion today over how safe we are from the coronavirus. What and who is the real threat to our safety? Our employees or the employers? Is the money in the bank enough? Will we be the next to receive the pink slip? And the airwaves, both national and international are back to saying, "The problem with India is its middle class. They are so fearful and self-serving that we can never have social change if we depend on them. They do not acknowledge their privilege and are therefore part of the problem."

It is no secret that India's growth rate spiked and so did her international image post-economic reforms. From a dowdy, meek, terribly diffident, and nice body language, Indians made the ballistic switch to designer wear and attitude, going so far as to begin to wear their provinciality with panache, some of it stoked by the "Dabangs and Piplis" from Bollywood. Nowhere was this metamorphosis more evident than on the cricket field where the polite guys of yore transformed into cocky, finger waggling images of defiance.

Today, when this newly confident middle class is blamed for being selfish and impervious to its social responsibility, I wonder at this surprising and misdirected demonization. In an interview on NDTV once, Javed Akhtar had trashed the trending "anger" of the middle class, calling it a very self-oriented and self-focused concern. He said the educated and professional India was supporting the Anna movement for her selfish reasons and that no one was actually bothered about the deprived and the poor. It is another matter and perhaps Javed Sa'ab is not aware, that a sizable number of these reviled middle class children are choosing to shun dazzling salaries for social activism, based in no mean measure upon a sense of security provided by the consolidation efforts of their parents.

It would therefore not be farfetched to say that this segment's "selfishness" in fact makes up the stable, productive, sane fabric of India. They are the class that harbor and nurture the "value system" of the nation. It is another matter that some WhatsApp groups today have become unsafe and unsavoury. These were supposed to be safe spaces of solidarity but are now broadcasting divisive content that some are hard put to trust. You either clap or beat utensils or you are against us.

It is unfair. India's middle class has had no help from any quarter. They are entirely self-made. They are also the component of India's population that stands the most to lose, with the greatest value at stake. It is their hard-earned prosperity that struggles to survive in the shadow of bribes and corruption and it is their peace of mind and a good night's sleep that thrashes around under the ever-present cloud of national guilt over India's disadvantaged.

What exactly have they done to create structural inequalities in society? Why are they blamed for poverty and deprivation in India? Granted that the reality has never been as stark as under the lockdown; so much so that the threat of the pandemic was overshadowed by large-scale hunger, homelessness, and dispossession of the working poor. Our social and economic blueprint is precarious, to say the least.

The simple question to ask: Is it people's selfishness or the policy paralysis that got us the Standard and Poor "junk rating?" The key to improving our SP rating is simple; clear the long-pending Parliamentary Bills, enforce our phenomenal laws, stop robbing the state coffers and leave the rest to India's middle class. Rather than vilify the golden goose, the country ought to work to make it easy and possible for more Indians to come into the fold of this enterprising and ambitious section.

Yes, the Resident Welfare Associations have been at war among themselves in the current crisis. The wages of domestic workers is being debated, their once-upon-a-time-indispensability being marvelled at. Do we even need them at all after managing for two months without them? The debates are endless and answers hard to come by. Are cloth masks good enough on morning walks? Ought vendors to be discriminated against based on religion? How to address the feeding of stray animals during the pandemic? Is vigilantism a civic issue?

Environment protection, a participatory democracy, the pacifist agenda, gender sensitivity, welfare state, human rights, arms reduction, energy renewal, terrorism management, nuclear policy; a whole lot is expected of the government and of each other. The powers better keep the fuel prices down, prevent earthquakes, assure our jobs and food security, make us proud citizens of a world power, and keep the enemy out. As enlightened citizens of the country, we are prepared to tell our government to spend our money with responsibility, represent our interest, and behave in a trustworthy manner. It is only a myth that the forms and systems cannot be restructured. Other democracies have been talking for years in terms of limiting serving terms and balancing budgets, shifting power to the states and setting up electronic citizen meetings, for starters.

May the middle class be sophisticated citizens of the world today? May it have so strong a sense of ties to the country and community that between a prayer for the nation and a reshaped public policy, they settle only and only for the latter!

Zoomer's Teacher

Primary teachers suffer from an inferiority complex. There is an inexplicable, implied, and rampant "dumbing" down of the profession. It is as though the vulnerability and perceived intellectual level of the students in their charge automatically pegs them alongside lab assistants, no offense meant. To add to this dowdy visage, there is the punishing class schedule that leaves them no time to be of any nuisance value.

Schools that practice the mother-teacher system in the Primary, place such an onus on the personal resources of the class teacher that she is done for, with the very first school bell. A typical Primary class teacher today handles the academic load of forty-odd children in addition to preparing daily absentee lists and keeping up with a battery of duties: bus, stay back, break duty. She is also a subject-in-charge, bulletin board-in-charge, and club-in-charge. There are records to be maintained such as the teacher's diary, attendance registers, bus attendance registers, gifted as well as remedial cases, assessment-related paraphernalia including report cards (online and hard copy), certificates, mark lists and not to mention the information booklets for the successive class teachers at the session end. There are the annual day and sports day rehearsals to get through. Quite a merry go round! They magically find the time to pack in a dozen seminars in a year and there are the staff welfare events to attend. Somewhere amidst this whirlwind day, a reasonable amount of effective teaching-learning is also to take place.

The 7th pay commission is supposed to justify all of this as also the accompanying ringing of the ears, spinning of the heads, and palpitating of the hearts. And it goes without saying that there is always that universal echo permeating the busy hullabaloo, "But what does the Primary teacher do the whole day?"

To begin with, the Primary is a world unto itself. A planet inhabited by raw, range of the moment, unique young people who are crying for validation and attention. It is not enough here to give them mere knowledge. They need and take a part of the teacher, if not a pound exactly. A good Primary teacher invests a lot of emotional energy in the classic manner she begins to identify with her class. This is a stake of a very personal nature. It is some of these crusading teachers who identify and nurture the wilting clovers, they back and showcase the tiger lilies, and they nudge and coax the humble heather. One has to hear that tinge of propriety in their tone when they say, "My class…."

Fortunately for this intrepid band, their love is returned in full measure. In many schools, the KG parent orientation marks that rite of passage, the switch of loyalties. It is understood that from thence on, the tots will heed their teacher more than they will, the counsel of their fathers and mothers. You have to see how they hang on their teacher's words, how they look at her as though they will lay their lives if asked. The flowers they make. The cards they painstakingly craft. Perhaps in a Primary teacher's life, her students are the only ones who say, "Ma'am, you are looking very beautiful today." They are loyal. They are a sight the day their teacher goes on leave. Of course, there are the odd fists pumping the air at the news but for the majority, there is a sense of sails deflating, a ship gone ashore, its anchor lost. Watch them how they follow their teacher blindly where she leads them.

And oh yes, they come back after years, looking for that one Primary teacher, their faces beaming up if she happens to remember their names.

It is here, in the Primary that you need the wisest, the kindest, and the most driven amongst the teaching community. Oddly enough, the enemy is within the ranks. It is not uncommon for colleagues to ask of a particularly high calibre teacher, "What are you doing here, wasting your time?"

And I have been one of this band once, many moons ago.

There were days when I would sit in a room full of high achieving professionals, many working at far greater levels of intellectual and financial remuneration and there would be this curious sense of pride. I could never keep the smile out of my reply when someone asked what I did for a living. I would find myself being very specific.

I wouldn't just say, "I am a teacher." For some reason, I liked to say "I am a Primary Teacher."

I taught the numerically gifted of Class 5. My eligibility? Well, let's say this assignment went a begging every year. Maths was not my favourite subject in school. But I would have you fooled those days.

When it was first suggested that I take this on, all I saw was the challenge, quietly telling myself I would figure it all out. It's another thing that my band of Number Crunchers believed I was born to teach the Fibonacci sequence.

They would troop into my Resource Centre every year, clutching their brand new Maths Club notebooks, a boxful of sharpened pencils under one arm, eyes a shade wide. They had been identified to possess an aptitude for the logical and had parents who declared wholehearted support for the program. Some were even familiar with the Soroban and Vedic Maths. Without losing much time and very soon at that, we would be a bunch, regularly biting off a whole lot more than we could chew.

We would start with the fascinating story of numbers. We marvelled at the audacity and clarity of the legendary Mathematical minds. There was a lot of scribbling, poring, and manipulating. I knew we were on track when I would begin to hear the long-suffering sighs of their class teachers as they watched the gigantic magic squares materialize on their green boards. Before long, this lot wanted to miss other activities to work on a puzzle or a pattern or a sequence. They would puff up their little torsos and prattle how zero was not "nothing" but an "absence of something". They would tell you a thing or two about the Sieve of Eratosthenes, rules of divisibility, painted cube question, pole in water working, and why we placed that darned x or 0 in double-digit multiplication; short of the universal truths…they were hearing a lot.

As we progressed, I would become the wiser too. I would realize how much the children loved to learn. They were intellectually resilient and quite up to the high demands placed on them. In fact, they mirrored you right back. There was something altogether unique about that class. Their similar aptitude; that ease with numbers, and the residence we are all forced to take, out of the box lent itself to a cohesive group effort. We made short shrift of several topics. I would begin in the lead but there would all too suddenly be these four feet geeks stamping all over my toes. We happily and routinely missed our play/break time to deal with worksheets. Inside my huge, well-lit centre, they were a maze of small heads bent over the Dienes' block but when I gazed up into space, I saw an array of outstanding professionals…there was a geomatics engineer, photogrammetrist, geodesist, environmental mathematician, robotics engineer, cryptologist, inventory strategist, an actuary, attorney, economist, and air traffic control analyst….as the capsule advanced, our alliance would become stronger. They would begin to appear at my door out of nowhere, "Ma'am, I have a doubt here."

The year would go by in a blur; the school was such a roller coaster of a place. Before long, I would be compiling a list of the mathematically inclined for the incoming sections. Another set of numbers happy! My graduating batch would by then have ridden into the senior wing's horizon until one fine day, during a regular Parent Teacher Meeting; I would sense a tall figure shuffling in my peripheral vision. Rohan! Precisely five years from when I first gaped at him, calculating in the air! That day I remember, he was clutching two papers.

I remember flipping the first over, it was a Maths question paper in Greek! As I reached out for the second, he leaned over shyly and pointed at his score in Maths. I looked up and saw his Dad in the shadows at the door.

I had trouble comprehending his paper but I could read the two smiles perfectly. It is hard to explain.

You have to be a Gen Z teacher to know that high.

Come Back, Hobbies

I am a boomer and I can knit, do crochet, macramé, and some decent tatting too. Oh, I forgot the cross stitch and lazy daisy work on Matty cloth and casement material. And remember the French knots!

How do you spend your free time millennial? Other than scrolling through Instagram, taking to Twitter, or browsing Netflix? You will blame the technology of course and perhaps you are right. But how do I tell you the joys of watching a bedcover take shape under your needlepoint? It breaks my heart that you will never know the sisterhood of sitting under a '*kikkar*' tree in Punjab with the womenfolk in the humid afternoons, humming folk songs, and knotting a '*dhurrie*' by hand. From scratch, let me tell you.

Yours is a generation submerged and swept away in your phones and social media. If it is not uploading, surfing, and taking shots of the screen, it is staring dopily at influencers and celebrities talk about their lives on Instagram. Where's yours? Life, I mean.

Siestas were frowned upon on the farms where I spent my school holidays. Call it hateful patriarchy but the girls were all skilled at hand churning for butter, stoking the cooking fire, scrubbing the brass utensils, and tending to the *tandoor*. We pitched in with serving the meals and the last round of thick, sweetened, piping pink milk. As a matter of fact, I tried my hand at milking the buffalo on occasions! Were we adequately stimulated? How high was our brain activity? What did our attention span look like? I just remember the high that comes from a task accomplished. Sure they were easy activities, fairly straightforward but what is so complicated about Instagram and Netflix? And yet they are not half as nourishing perhaps as reading, cooking, or sewing.

Come on, admit it. You have lost the hobbies. It is just about the hustle now, side or main. Everything has to be a moneymaking enterprise. How about some creative handiwork that is guaranteed to bring you a sense of joyful accomplishment, peace, and real relaxation? How about borrowing patterns from each other? How about sharing notes on half-stitch and double-stitch? How about knitting a snug cap for a loved one?

Hobbies have all but died out. There is just binge-watching one hears of and through the night. How exhausting, the flickering screen that carries you away from your own reality! There lies an entire alternate world of not just instant joy but also long-term personal development through hobbies. In this life so full of the daily humdrum obligations, hobbies block you your "you" time. Giving yourself some creative tasks outside of long working hours is full of benefits for your mental health and wellbeing. Direct benefits of hobbies go beyond the physical such as through exercise, dance, and movement. These wholesome pursuits can leave you feeling empowered through creative freedom and cognitive focus such as the ability to concentrate on a pleasurable activity without the day-to-day interruptions of life.

There are other indirect benefits of hobbies such as a sense of achievement and goals, new learning experiences, increased social contact, and formation of new connections. Most of my life's enduring friendships have been through shared interests. I have my horse-riding mates with whom I have had the unimaginable fortune of riding on hunts over the Ooty downs. There are my golf buddies that have given me memories of daybreak tee-offs followed by piping hot coffee. What would I be without my Spanish language classmates bonding over tension-filled orals!

Millennials and Zoomers, you simply have to turn to hobbies to help with your general wellbeing. Stop looking at your phone for stimulation. There are plenty of other ways to switch off from the hustle and bustle of daily life and fill your hours with. Those darned phones can contribute to anxiety and depression, but hobbies can provide the perfect antidote to stress. With reason! You see, hobbies require an individual to focus solely on whatever it is they're doing, putting other thoughts out of their mind for a few minutes or hours — which is ultimately the definition of mindfulness and meditation. There are tremendous mental health benefits of taking up hobbies. Take up rock-climbing. Join a cycling group. Get into drawing Mandala paintings. There is a virtual sea of skills out there, for the taking. I have tried my hand at Zumba, Yoga, Bollywood dancing, Garba lessons, Waltz, and Tango at various stages of life.

At regular intervals, I pick up a new skill project. Keeping at this consistently has helped me rack up a hamper of skills that give me the confidence to be at home anywhere in the world. If it was learning to swim the freestyle one season, it was cycling 100 km in another. If the aim was to sharpen my golf score during one phase it became all about learning to play the Greensleeves on the piano in another. I have laboured over my bachata and rock-n-roll. I have burnt the midnight oil over the conjugations of Spanish language. I have taught myself the backstroke and butterfly in swimming. Bit by bit, a step at a time…I learned the habit of stepping out of my comfort zone.

Don't be afraid. Don't do a cost-benefit analysis. Don't bother about perfecting a skill. Don't look too far ahead. There's something for every interest and budget out there, whether it's baking, sketching, home-brewing, photography or hiking. So, how do you spend your free time? If the answer concerns you, it's not too late to make a change. Bring back simple-yet-fun hobbies for 2021 and stop technology drowning you out.

Death from Work

How does the younger generation in Japan view the nation's famed extreme work-culture?

Well, there was a grassroots effort at Osaka recently. A 'memorial service' was held and led by a Buddhist priest to 'mourn' the missed moments and lapsed leave given up by Japan's holiday-hungry labor force. Hundreds of lanterns were lit and released with poignant messages of regret from the workers.

"My child's birthday party was delayed by seven months," read one message.

Another said, "I could not say goodbye to my grandparents after they died."

And, "I reached retirement age without using 90% of leave every year".

Shiboru Yamane, creative director at Ningen Inc, the Osaka-based advertising production company behind the event, explains: "We wanted people to visualize what they could be doing with their paid leave through these lanterns. In many cases, a harsh work environment leads to mental health issues and even death. It's a very big problem in Japan."

There is a stunning piece of literature that evokes perspectives for just such a debate. 'The Remains of the Day' is a 1989 historical novel by the Nobel Prize-winning British author Kazuo Ishiguro. The protagonist, Stevens, is a butler with a long record of service at Darlington Hall, a stately home near Oxford, England. In 1956, he takes a road trip to visit a former colleague and reminisces about events at Darlington Hall in the 1920s and 1930s.

The work received the Man Booker Prize for Fiction in 1989. A film adaptation came in 1993 starring Anthony Hopkins and Emma Thompson. It was nominated for eight Academy Awards.

The butler's lonely musings involve reflection on a life given over to a single moral principle: loyalty to his boss. His sacrifices and their consequences for him and others paint a terrifying picture of a moral code taken to extremes.

'Karoshi', or death from overwork, is an ongoing issue within Japan's excessive work culture. It is high on the agenda of Prime Minister Shinzo Abe too, as reflected in the government's new Work Style Reform Bill, which was passed by Japan's national legislature in 2018. It went into effect the following April. The bill is a cornerstone of his attempts to modernize Japan's way of working — known as *hataraki-kata kaikaku* in Japanese — with amendments to eight key labour laws. Initiatives range from caps on excessive working hours to increased flexibility, as well as a requirement for employees to designate at least five days off work for staff with at least 10 days of unused leave.

Highlighting the government's goal of boosting rates of taken annual leave to 70% in 2020, Susumu Oda, director of the Work and Life Harmonisation Division at the Ministry of Health, Labour and Welfare, explains: "It has been recognized that gaining time off work is important to refresh employees both mentally and physically."

Now Japan's managers were rated the least likely to approve worker leave in a study surveying 19 countries. Is it any wonder that according to the most recent government figures only 52.4% of the workers took the paid leave to which they were entitled in 2018? The main reason is said to be guilt –it's considered normal for workers to take the last train home every night. And apparently the words "Japan" and "holiday" rarely feature in the same sentence. Not taking holiday leave is a normalized part of working life. No one thinks about the impact on the family, health, or wellbeing of the worker. The workplace atmosphere does not allow taking time off from work. The workers do not take off even when they are sick. The managers work late and so do the subordinates, no one wants to be the only one taking leave. It is not unusual for some to "not check" their leave entitlement even.

Younger generations increasingly are pushing back against their nation's dangerous workplace customs. There already exist 1 million or more *hikikomori* in Japan today, most of these social recluses spending years, sometimes decades, in isolation. Unsuited to Japanese work culture, one of them cited sleep deprivation and overwork at a game company he entered following graduation as the trigger for his shut-in behaviour. Isolating at home helped him to recalibrate his life.

It is challenging however to change Japan's work habits; they are too deeply engrained. In a Vacation Deprivation study on annual leave in workforces around the world from Expedia, the travel booking company, Japan scored lowest among 19 countries and regions in its 2018 study, with workers taking on average only half their annual leave — 10 days out of 20. As many as 58% of Japanese workers cited "feeling guilty" as the main reason for not taking their entitled holiday leave in the 2018 Expedia report, with only 43% stating that their employer was supportive of them taking leave — the lowest globally.

The fewer days taken off by Japanese employees in traditional companies, the better standing they have with their managers and co-workers.

There is a clear gap between generations though. Akina Murai, head of PR for Expedia in Japan says, "62% of Japanese aged 18 to 34 are feeling vacation deprived, compared to only 40% of over-50s. This generation gap shows that although the younger employees want and see the need to take more vacation, they are challenged by their superiors who do not think or operate in the same manner."

While the Work Style Reform Bill is being described as a "huge step in the history of Japanese labour law", the low rate of taken holiday leave is just one element among many that need addressing in order to modernize the nation's work culture. To bring about real change, factors being highlighted are the importance of tackling the nation's dwindling birth-rate and supporting paternity leave to creating a workforce that is more accommodating to women and the elderly.

Japan is starting to change. However, this change is not easy. Shinjiro Koizumi, Japan's environment minister, faced widespread opposition and even calls to resign over his plans to take paternity leave after his wife gave birth. Hope, however, can be found in the form of younger workers, who are increasingly rejecting the overworked path of older generations of salarymen.

It's very hard not to read the novel "Remains of the day" at least in part as a cautionary tale about the limits of loyalty and the points at which we start to lose ourselves in our jobs.

Public Display of Affection

We arrived home from the movie *Ishaqzaade*.

On the face of it, a usual and the regular outing for us empty nesters, going to the movies. But this particular viewing turned out to be different, ending up becoming an experience in fact.

For one, we chose to go to "Delite Diamond" on Aruna Asif Ali Road to watch this flick. It is a very different world from the DT Star Promenade. The crowds wait outside on the pavement until the hall has been emptied of the previous show. The popcorn is cheaper and less buttery, the coffee frothier, and sprinkled with chocolate powder. People are aggressively unapologetic, answering cell phones in loud, completely at home voices. No one bats an eyelid when annoying voices are raised at audible conversations.

There were several sideshows in progress inside the hall, running parallel to the drama on screen. When the movie broke at intermission, for instance, there came in a harassed looking man, shuffling up to the last row where we were seated. He did not look like he owned a movie ticket. There was in his hand a tiny digital camera instead. After a momentary hesitation, he took quick and furtive pictures of the couple sitting two seats down the row, to my right. There was a muted flurry, a subdued, almost calm suspense, broken eventually by the lady who squeezed past my feet, grazing them slightly, to go and stand near the photographer. A couple of urgent voiced exchanges later, it was established that the photographer was indeed her husband who had come to confront her being cosy with her office boyfriend! I gaped as she walked out of the hall and her husband lowered himself next to the much younger Lochinvar to ask him outright and distinctly so, "Are you having an affair with my wife? I want to know. I have a five-year-old son." The paramour says, "No, no…there is no such thing." Just like that!!

A young couple entered late, again to my right! She wore a comprehensive *hijab* over her face, covering it all but for the eyes. The cover came off completely just as soon as they were settled into the far corner. The two proceeded to bond over intermittent lunges and a heart to heart dialogue, treating the movie hall more as a safe getaway than a space with any clear purpose. One of their phones would suddenly begin flashing as they pored over some mutually gratifying photographs

This is new India, I told myself bemusedly.

Far more than anything else, there was a dissonant pathos in these alternative lives unfolding around us. In their needs, clearly on display, there shone a reflection of what lay at home. The movie hall was many things to many people. A comfortable, air-conditioned break for the policeman on duty, an escape from drudgery and despair for the adventurous lady, and a cosy cove for the young couple.

Interestingly, the images on screen spun a similar story of the small-town life in India. Against a realistic location of small landfills, grubby rail tracks, grimy toilets, sweaty and unkempt humanity, *Zoya* and *Parma* lived their curiously escapist existence. I saw a certain menace in *Parma's* filial obedience and loyalty. His childish and short-range reactions were as though, cries of defiance against the terrifying violence around him. *Zoya's* inner world was unravelling, even more, make-believe, if anything. From being a filmy and pampered daughter, she was cast out of the family in a cruel turn of events. Her unrealistic flights of fancy with *Parma* were chilling in their disconnect with what lay around her. There was sexism, there were clichés, there was a predictable end but most of all, there was a deep-seated desolation in the jagged frames of *Ishaqzaade*. They spoke of people dying to live, of hating to love, of defying to die.

For me, the predominant flavour of the film was one of no places to go, no cause for hope, and no silver lining to the cloud. In the movie's dim-lit fabric lay a tale of chronic clan wars, deliberately cultivated male chauvinism and the validation of might being right. The only bugle belonged to the male heads of the *Chauhan* and *Quereshi* families, the rest provided the shell for their mounting.

Ishaqzaade had seemed like the dead-end of small-town India. It was not about living but about staying alive.

The following morning I was at the Lodhi gardens where the young couples sat wrapped up in their bubbles? They remained frozen for hours together, moving barely and even then, solely for greater angular access to the other. The hour this spectacle unfolded was about 11 am stretching well into the lunch hours and beyond.

I know because those were the winter months of Delhi's mellow sun and I loved walking in its forenoon snugness. The lovebirds sat cheek by jowl, whispering, gazing, peering into their mobiles occasionally. There were tears sometimes. The girl would wear that feminine expression of aggrieved anguish, the boy leaning in closer as though to reassure.

I tried not to stare. I stole quick glances through my photochromatic frames and around my sports Bluetooth earphones. But the drama was compelling. On one of those days, I nearly missed my step at a desi lip-lock taking place right in my path. I looked away in haste then flicked my eyes back just to make sure this indeed was happening in broad daylight and in the public gaze.

India had never before been so much in love! And because I was such an Aunty my mind went to the parents of these lovelorn pairs. What were they told about their children's coordinates? Did they think their kids were at college or some coaching class? They looked too carefree to be employed anywhere. The earth seemed to have come to a stop for them. They were entirely and wholly in the moment.

I almost envied them for their meditative leisure. Then my thoughts went gallivanting in another direction. They were probably emotionally illiterate. Did they know that a healthy couple love looks nothing like in the movies? That a certain form of exclusivity could be toxic. But again, that could have just been modern love. Caught up yes but convenient above everything else.

Millennial's Envy

There is a new profession in town. Criticism! A destructive, no holds barred tearing down of people who are on the rise in their respective fields. And nowhere is it as visible as in the creative arts and the media.

Take Barkha Dutt. Currently busy covering COVID-19 on the streets of India, she fuels an entire industry of noxious denigration. A website called MediaCrooks once placed her at number one on their list of India's worst journalists. If you looked closely, the reasons given were Radiagate, the alleged Kargil and 26/11 journalistic misadventures, her propensity for Pakistan and Rahul Gandhi, and the fact that she is the only journalist purported to have a "wardrobe sponsor". The rest was a lot of words.

Now Barkha Dutt happens to be a "Padma Shri". She was nominated in 2011 with Sir Richard Attenborough and Ross Kemp for the "International TV Personality of the Year". She is also a member of the National Integration Council of India and has been an accomplished conflict zone reporter and TV talk show hostess. About 7 plus million people follow her on twitter. She writes a weekly column, has interviewed a range of personalities, was the subject of a Bollywood movie, and has won umpteen national and international awards.

'Barkha Rani Jamke Barasti Hai', it says on her twitter profile. She is an Emmy nominated reporter, columnist @ Washington Post, and a self-described 'Yaaron Ka Yaar'.

This speaks of a huge body of work, by any standards, and spanning only twenty plus years.

An objective, fact-based, professional criticism would have been understandable but downright muckiness forces one to wonder what exactly is at play here. I read some more and found the author claim at one point that on the stated charter of Mediacrooks, "….there were hundreds of provisions to identify and talk about the crooks but not a single one to identify the good ones or the best in the business."

So there you are, the online destruction stood justified in view of their mission which was to identify the crooks. And what did they do if they did not find any; they manufactured one!

During a "We the People" episode on clinical trials in 2012, I began a tweet exchange with Barkha Dutt on her bright yellow dupatta and this is how it evolved:

@BDUTT Lovely yellow dupatta! Potential add on to your signature, a vibrant colour every time but then Mediacrooks will allege distraction.

@Honeysangha:))) ha ha do you really pay any attention to them. Thanks:)

@BDUTT Hard put to escape the 24/7 spew emanating from these practitioners of the latest profession in town; criticism for its own sake.

@Honeysangha indeed! but I just block and couldn't care less:-)

@BDUTT This is the age of dis-information or black propaganda. Wise to rebut or to ignore? Ten people call the rose a weed and that it is!

@Honeysangha disagree completely. If that's what it takes for a rose to be a weed, so be it. Who cares!

@BDUTT Cheers to that self-assured dismissal! Wish you many more such tweets of well-earned certainty!!

@Honeysangha:))thankee

Now I am a Barkha Dutt fan and had hastened to conclude the above exchange on a positive note but the thought that disinformation needed to be addressed lingered.

I believe there are two categories of people where work is concerned. One kind commits, the other comments; one burns the midnight oil, the other burns their hearts; one has no time or inclination to look around, while that is all the other is doing; one is foolish, the other foolhardy.

There is more. The good workers invariably come wired with a deep-seated arrogance that blinds them to the hooks dangling in the vicinity. So strong is their faith in personal merit, they are either shocked at or outright dismissive of destructive criticism. Neither is effective. In the excessively networked world, we inhabit today, there is no escaping connection. Black propaganda exists and the sheer range and reach of digital media puts it out of the harmlessness of just a couple of people talking rubbish. Disinformation today infects the ether, resounds back into the atmosphere, and circles the globe, tearing reputations, undermining good work, and leading to huge wastes of human endeavour.

Disinformation deserves to be beaten back. A responsible online conduct needs to be canvassed. We ought to care that so much hate is snaking around the web links. Adults, kids, everybody who gets online needs to be watchful, critical, and analytical. Is the website genuine? What is their purpose of existence? Is the information they post accurate, current, and comparable?

That there are so many disinformation artists and agents clogging the net-ways is hardly reason enough to give up the desire to hear and speak the truth. Silence can be a very deadly sanction!

But the world is kinder today. It is expected to be at any rate. Witches burn, children starve, civilians perish in wars, women are raped but not without protest. There is a strong pretence at civil liberties; an educated progressiveness that is synonymous with a repugnant horror at inhumanity and injustice; to that extent, we have evolved as a species. But does this all also make the Millennials any less envious as a generation? Does the green-eyed monster lurk within them?

In "The Age of Envy," Ayn Rand defined envy as "hatred of the good for being the good."

Since the best antidote for envy — for the hatred of the good for being the good — is considered always to love the good, Ayn Rand puts it into words at the conclusion of "The Age of Envy."

"What is the weapon one needs to fight such an enemy? For once, it is I who will say that love is the answer — love in the actual meaning of the word, which is the opposite of the meaning they give it — love as a response to values, love of the good for being the good. If you hold on to the vision of any value you love — your mind, your work, your wife or husband, or your child — and remember that that is what the enemy is after, your shudder of rebellion will give you the moral fire, the courage and the intransigence needed in this battle. What fuel can support one's fire? Love for man at his highest potential."

High School Dating

The judge's chair during a junior wing dance competition gets increasingly uncomfortable. I sit there fiddling with my pen and staring at the score sheet. The costume is authentic, the synchrony is great, the stage has been used well but the lyrics of the song are age-inappropriate and so are the expressions and the accompanying body thrusts. There is, "*Darling aankho se aankhe chaar hone do*" and "*Desi girl*" and "*Jhumka gaira re*" and "*Chad gayo papi bicchua*" even "*Atharra baras ki main hone ko aayee.*"

Sure, it is easy to indulgently dismiss the butterball reproduction of raunchy, Bollywood choreography. The tubbies do look cute in adult finery, although the eye pauses on the blouse strings and lack of them. To make it tougher to protest, the audience is quick on the trigger, precisely on these dubious numbers, clapping and joining in with a hearty chorus. I have pinched myself and turned 360 degrees to try and catch the eyes of the other seniors sitting there. Some do shake their heads slowly but quite a few wear a mock stern expression, barely hiding the twinkle in the eye.

So, the competition moves on, in the same gear. Year after year, grade after grade. The beginning is well-intentioned. Class teachers are told to discourage their students from turning in performances based on suggestive music. One particularly concern filled year, a blanket ban was implemented on all filmy song and dance. The participation plunged to an alarming low. There were in fact, some protests from the parents! Many were not equipped to assist their children in the preparation; the TV eased the preparatory rehearsal somewhat. And so, we had these little ones, stumbling up to the music table with their CDs of Lady Gaga and Rihanna. I would shudder inwardly, wondering at the deadly music video images that had to be streaming through the tiny heads when the notes of these worthies came on.

There is almost an anaesthetic social numbness to age and grace inappropriate sexual messages? So desensitized is the air that anything and everything seems to go. We are completely blind to what this irregular acceptance is doing to our children. In fact, we are joining in. I have to admit, that I swung to both the *Sheila* and *Munni* numbers with our Fifth graders, during a school camp. I am certain that the volume the DJ was playing the songs at, was rendering the lyrics quite inconsequential; we mostly stayed with the beat. This is no justification, but naturally.

The question is not about sexuality per se but of a version that does not go well with a certain chronological, mental, and emotional level of growth.

There is something else palpable and alien, rearing, and growing up in our schools. It is the increasingly acknowledged phenomenon of dating. An entirely new and unfamiliar frontier for all concerned, this high school culture is cocking a huge snook at the hitherto acceptable definitions and parameters of teen discipline, safety, and security.

What used to be spoken of in hushed undertones gets progressively audible as teachers, parents, and staff members watch young people pushing the envelope, literally. Coming upon unexpected incidents of intimacy do not shock anymore and it is fairly de rigueur to have the educational spaces populated by dopey looking couples, shuffling in an invisible pink bubble, wearing school uniforms. It is as though the entire dynamics of the school system has swung from performance-based self-worth to relationships-oriented wellbeing. Watch that awkward spring to their steps and a shy voltage around them, you can't miss it.

There used to be such a stigma attached to even a hint of these engagements in the past that one has to stop and wonder at the currently charged academic environment. What do these relationships signify in a time and space that is primarily earmarked for learning and value addition? How is this emotional maze impacting one of the most impressionable and vulnerable segments of our population? At a phase in life when they should be completely focused on their own development and growth, is it doing them any good to draw their self-esteem from amorous equations with other young people as wet behind the ears as they themselves?

I feel concerned at this new-fangled world of relationships where closeness is illusory, based as it is on instant communication powered by text messaging and Google talk. There is no distance or breathing space to reflect on the friendship as the young lurch from one emotional strife to another, hanging out or hooking up. There is a real danger of jealous and controlling behaviour being mistaken for love. And how about the other, gender-based issues of unrealistic demands being made on either or partner? With the adolescent's need for autonomy and high dependence on peers, dating violence and sexual assault go unreported for the most part. As of now, there seems to be nothing in the way of their first line of defence moreover. Truth be told, we are all in a blissful state of denial, shaking our heads and saying that this problem is exaggerated.

It is not. There is a real, clear, and present world of sexual hostility out there in our schools. It ought to be addressed with a stated policy on gender discrimination and sexual assault by individual institutions. We are not talking statistics and case histories here, these are real people, our friends, students, acquaintances, and family members who are struggling with overwhelming emotions and pressures. The first thing to do is to call attention to it, to report it so that it does not go unpunished or unnoticed.

Too many young people are thrashing about in whirlpools of confusing signals with no clear roadmaps from adults who refuse to look their way from their spots in the sand. Schools have an obligation to promulgate policy, related handling procedures, and necessary disciplinary action to deal with such incidents. Mere standing guard and physical vigilance is not good enough just as it does not help to call parents and engage in mutual blaming. These are civil rights we are talking about, the right of a student to receive instruction in a safe, comfortable, and non-threatening space. Adults in charge of the young cannot use the excuse of having no knowledge of their adventurism to escape accountability.

Sexual harassment starts with standing in the basketball grounds and rating the other gender on a scale of ten. First comes the acknowledgement of its existence and then educating students on what is healthy and what is not; what is safe and what is not; what is empowering and what will damage them for life.

To Snap or No

Snapchat, the photo-messaging app has been flexing its muscles in India. The app has seen a phenomenal user jump. Not only has the team been growing in the country, but there has also been talk of developing culturally relevant products, community engagement, and partnerships. This has involved the launching of support in five more languages, there has been an introduction of creative tools to celebrate cultural moments and festivals; celebrities such as Taapsee Pannu have been taken on board as a Snap Star.

What exactly does the app do? It allows users to share photos with friends for a limited period of time after which the content disappears. The sender gets to decide how long a photo will "live," from one to 10 seconds, after it's viewed. There are filters and lenses on offer, many of which are augmented reality-enabled. In fact, this is the fundamental way Snapchat engages its users. In other words, an enhanced version of reality is possible by overlaying digital information on an image for instance. In fact, the first Lensathon in partnership with Skillenza was concluded as recently as the 22 May this year. Lensathon is an online hackathon where participants create eye-catching lenses and AR or augmented reality experiences using Lens Studio by Snap.

In the year gone by, the company hosted 11 Lens Studio workshops in colleges and universities in India. With the COVID-19 pandemic going on, these sessions are being hosted virtually this year in conjunction with some premier professional schools.

What makes Snapchat so popular? The happiness involved in editing, filtering, and fooling around with goofy pictures, doodles, bitmojis, crazy filters, and other creative effects. There is a snappy snapping happening with this app. A "must-have app" among teens and tweens, it is winning over some older adults too. A whimsy way to the consumer's heart, Snapchat offers you a way to display digital versions of yourself and your friends in a fun way. And even though, there is a base age prerequisite of 13 years of age, how is the administration going to keep track?

The way to add friends is by username, address book, Snapcode or users nearby. Others can add you similarly. Once added, both can view all of each other's content on Snapchat. There is a false sense of security that users can send embarrassing or plain silly time-limited photos without fear of them landing up on other social media sites where they are sure to live on forever. The problem is that there are ways to capture and recover images sent even as snaps. To Snapchat's credit, if a receiver takes a screenshot of the photo, the sender is notified, but that may not be enough to prevent the photo from being shared later with others. In addition, if a receiver knows that a message is coming, they could take a photo of the screen with another phone or digital camera and the sender would never know that their supposedly evaporating photo would be alive and well on someone else's device.

Snapchat was developed by Evan Spiegel and Bobby Murphy, two Stanford University students who felt emoticons weren't sufficient to convey human emotions in their entirety but there was wariness over the expressive snaps ending up on social media for the whole wide world to see. Here is where the idea of a time-limited photo-sharing application was born.

Snapchat is wildly popular. Consider these stats, compiled by Omnicore:

In 2020, Snapchat had an average of 218 million daily active users that generated over three billion snaps a day.

Active Snapchatters open the app 30 times a day.

More than 60 percent of active Snapchatters create new content on a daily basis.

On average, users spend 49.5 minutes a day on Snapchat and send 34.1 messages a day.

There are however parental concerns about issues of compromising the safety of the users. Since Snapchat doesn't save pictures and messages sent parents cannot effectively monitor the smartphone use by their children. And teens have been known to be tempted to use Snapchat for "sexting." Snapchat itself admits that up to 25% of users may send sensitive content on a regular basis "experimentally." This can lead to the all-too-common occurrence of being bullied.

There are some other features that ought to be discussed with young users. Introduced in 2017, Snap Map allows users to share their location in real-time with anyone on their Snapchat friend list and see the locations of their friends who do the same. This is alright only so long as all their Snapchat contacts are real friends, otherwise, there is a big risk involved. Launched in 2015, the Discover feature allows you to see content from popular media channels like MTV, Cosmopolitan, Vice, and BuzzFeed — many of which offer sexually oriented content.

Then there are the Snapstreaks that occur when two users have snapped back and forth within a 24-hour period for three days in a row. For many kids, they're a measure of their friendships. There are concerns however that the pressure of keeping a streak going, particularly many at a time may take a toll on kids. Snapchat interactions are as close as we can get to physical interactions within the social media realm. And each piece of content is expected to be raw, in-the-moment authentic and natural footage, just as physical interactions are. Every Snap doesn't need to be planned or perfect; it just needs to be real.

Snapchat can be a fun and engaging app when used appropriately, carefully, and with very specific ground rules. The app has a potential for problems like sexting, cyberstalking, and cyberbullying though. It makes you wonder if the cons outweigh the pros here. But the key with Snapchat, as with all platforms of social media, is to educate yourself on what you or your child are getting into. It's not about what apps you or your kids are using — it's about how the apps are being used and understood.

Gen Z's Watershed Moment

Towards the end of last year, there was a face-off at home. Our millennial daughter was demanding that we pick up the phone to mobilize medical help for young university students protesting against the controversial Citizenship (Amendment) Act (CAA). She was inconsolable and in tears over her friends having to face the brunt of police brutalities. The updates were coming thick and fast over the social media and I remember facing her frustration at our inertia one night. She could not fathom how her parents could just sit there unmoving while young people were out on the roads raising slogans in solidarity with their injured colleagues. Eventually, our two girls gave up on their pro-establishment boomer parents and left home with packed sandwiches and coffee to stake the night out at the scene of action.

I remember my mixed feelings. On the one hand, I was petrified for their safety, and on the other, I felt a fierce pride in their response to the agitation. I had myself taken them to the Ramlila grounds during the anti-corruption agitation of 2011, which led to the formation of a new political outfit, the Aam Aadmi Party (AAP). At the time I had wanted them to experience the real dynamics of democracy at work. They have since been poised and ready to jump into social and political action in the public spaces. And now they have been joined by the Gen Z.

Generation Z or Gen Z is the term used to describe the generation of young men and women reaching adulthood at the end of the second decade of the 21st-century. In other words, anyone born in 1995 and onwards. And India has the world's largest Generation Z. According to UN projections, there are currently 99.2 million Gen Z adults, aged between 18 and 22 years. This is roughly a fifth of the world's entire Gen Z cohort, a proportion greater than China, the US, and Europe.

The growing importance of this generation is reflected not just in these protests and rallies but also on the internet. Google searches for the Gen Z peaked in 2019. This cohort was born into technology. They are like fish in internet water. They are so at home with social media that it has earned them the stereotype of being tech-addicted, anti-social, or "social justice warriors." This lot will very soon become pivotal to the future of retail. In fact, many of them are expected to have a sizable spending power by 2026.

But Gen Zers are different from older generations; their bar for how they spend their time online is higher, their weapons of choice being the photo-sharing app Instagram and the short video sharing app TikTok. There are other differences as per the most recent YouGov-Mint Millennial Survey. This generation is considered to be a bit more political and "woke" as compared to their predecessors. Around 25% of Gen Z adults (18–22 years) said they had participated in some form of protests and rallies compared to 22% among Millennials.

Not only is Generation Z more tolerant than other generations, but they are also more concerned with unemployment and women's safety. Family, work, and time for themselves came across as the most important factors for Gen Z. Relative to the older generations, they also tend to hold liberal views on the most important social issues. Sadly enough, an overwhelming majority among the Gen Z believe it is difficult to find a job these days. Given the current circumstances, these anxieties are only going to grow and cause instability if left unaddressed.

Gen Z has some crazy coming of age stories. There is one of Anirudh Gandotra dropping out of college at the age of 19 to be on his own. In other words, flirt with some startup ideas before moving on to something more concrete. He eventually built his own app-based content platform. There is another of Jasjeet Singh who happened to fall asleep during his semester exam in the third year of B Com and never went back to college after that day. One internship after another followed concluding in a tenure with a seed and accelerator program for early-stage start-ups.

While the Millennials grew up during an economic boom, this generation came to age during a recession. Their pragmatism is a foil to the idealism of the Millennials. Where the name of the game for Millennials was having experiences, Gen Z would rather save money. And even as the Millennials prefer brands that share their values, Gen Z would rather use brands that feel authentic.

Gen Z is beginning early at work, they are figuring it out real fast and want to build things and create an impact. Their tools are internet credentials and personal branding. What gets them going is money and titles. Are the employers ready for this freshly minted workforce?

"Organisations have to change with the times," said Ganesh S Iyer, CEO of Symphony Ventures India, whose team has more than 50 Gen Z-ers, most of whom are engineers. "Few things have definitely changed over the last few years: Gen Z wants much more clarity on the expected role and if that does not fit into their worldview, they will refuse the role. They are very clear about what they want. Also, a lot more tech-based hiring tools have evolved and Gen Z is extremely comfortable using them. And work-life balance is sacrosanct for Gen Z. They also give importance to instant gratification in terms of rewards, career growth, or a raise," Iyer said.

What will work best with Gen Z is an explanation of the purpose behind decisions. It would help too to give their requirements a conscious listen. Employers will also have to map their careers as the future is about individual skill-building.

They face their watershed moment with the pandemic. Predictions are that they will emerge from this with a high level of stress over events involving large groups of people. Given the masks and headphones that blunt identity, expression, and interaction, they may end up creating new signs and signals for relating from behind masks. They are also expected to grow up being less coddled, what with parents stressed out over lost jobs and full-time parenting. Expectations are that they will step in and vote for change. As communities repeatedly open up, encounter danger, and close down again as the virus mutates and reoccurs, Gen Z digs in harder into the home scene. They will value the security of home. Gen Zs have often been called Globals for their inclusive, world-wide outlook, and they have always been a fundamentally urban generation. That will change. They will travel less and see fewer foreign countries.

Today, Gen Z looks to us as parents and grandparents, as educators, community leaders, and policymakers. It is up to us, to Gen X, Boomers and Millennials to model resilience, create community, and be protective of our link to the future.

The Snake People

Have you heard of the Snake People? They are none other than our Millennials!

Here is what happened. Coder Eric Bailey, a millennial, of course, age 32, got so tired of seeing headlines speaking of his generation as though they were "this weird, dehumanized, alien phenomenon," as he put it, in an interview with The Wall Street Journal, he decided to own the portrayal. The idea was to fight back with online mockery. And he did. By creating a browser extension that changed the word "Millennials" to "snake people" anytime it appeared online. He told the Huffington Post: "It started off as a joke to myself. I was like: Who the hell would want this?" The winking claim was that it "reveals the *real* truth behind" the loosely defined, much-discussed generation.

The perceived hurt at being cast as some sort of an uncomplimentary cultural stereotype is not imaginary. I have two Millennials at home, chafing at the bit at regular intervals. The snake people extension extended to other events involving the Millennials. Occupy Wall Street, for instance, became the "Great Ape-Snake War."

The browser extension was launched in 2015. It had developed a strong following which really took off after The New York Times ran an amusing correction to a fact-check piece on President Trump's claims on trade deficits. "Because of an editing error involving a satirical text-swapping web browser extension, an earlier version of this article misquoted a passage from an article by the Times reporter Jim Tankersley. The sentence referred to America's narrowing trade deficit during 'the Great Recession,' not during 'the Time of Shedding and Cold Rocks.' (Pro tip: Disable your 'Millennials to Snake People' extension when copying and pasting.)"

Some of the headlines have since read like these:

"Dear Snake People, We're Sorry."

"Almost half of snake people tweet while they eat, survey says."

"Most snake people OK taking confidential files home."

"Do snake people want to get married?"

"TEENS: Snake people: A political powerhouse."

"How becoming a mom changes the snake people's buying and media habits."

"7 facts every business should know about snake people".

"4 ways my butt helps engage snake people at work."

"When you've been hanging out with too many snake people bro."

The question being asked by those that dabble in psychology is, "Was this extension, deep down, an act of self-loathing? Have we reached the point where snake people wish to shed their skin and admit who they really are?" Who are they? It is the Generation Y that is better known as Millennials; those reaching young adulthood around the year 2000. Oh yes, they don't buy cars or houses, they communicate primarily through text heavy with emojis and they also periodically congregate at EDM (Electronic Dance Music) "concerts". They experience difficulty looking someone in the eye when talking to them. They often live at home and would rather hang out with friends than invest their free time in their 20's on a worthwhile career.

In defence of the boomers, there is something compelling about a group of young people who work through the witching hour and constantly talk of chilling and lacking bandwidth for selective mundane tasks. It is almost sinister, their talk of the meaning of life and a deep interest in saving the world, never mind the mess in their immediate surroundings. It is bewildering; their ever-present itch to escape into the hills, to get away from it all. It seems almost contemptible that given the servings of life they received on a platter, they think nothing of admitting they did not ask to be born. Even though they may have contributed to being maligned, they may not be faulted for it, that's the way of the snake people.

So, if you're not particularly worried about giving Chrome plugins permission to "read and change all your data on the websites you visit," go ahead and try installing the Millennials to Snake People extension. It merely follows in the footsteps of a handful of similar extensions that playfully "fix" the language of the Internet. In the final analysis, neither Millennials to Snake People nor Millennials Begone! are making fun of the generation they pretend to mock. Instead, what they are doing is parodying the way the media reports on the Millennials.

What else are these attempts to classify, characterize, and generalize but empty gestures of control? When there is naming and describing happening, there is someone trying to regulate. Human history is rife with several other examples of social stereotyping that has occasionally been wrested by the target group, remember the Slut-Walks around the world that just decided to claim the word 'slut'.

Each historical cohort has its own "flavor", and each cohort, in turn, irritates the ones that came before. The older members of the Millennial cohort call themselves Xennials (pronounced "zennial") to show that they are in some ways caught between Gen X and Millennials. This cohort graduated before smartphones and social media were standard teenage accessories. All of their high school and college relationships were conducted IRL (in real life) and not showcased on social media.

The Millennials may annoy the older generation, but they are doing exactly what they are supposed to do—they are trying to find their own way. They are trying to figure out what kind of world they want to create as their legacy. Perhaps they need the time and the space to build a vision and make that all-important difference.

How about we exercise some generational empathy and give our Millennials a break and let them have a chance to find their way and show us their version of our shared future. Gen Z after all, is already nipping at their heels!

And if nothing else, Millennials to Snake People is good for a laugh or two. But if you install it, be warned: You may need to ask a snake person how to remove it from your browser. Here then is to the time-honoured tradition of the generation gap and er...well...adulting!

OK Gen Z

Generations at the core are pretty much a form of cultural diversity. These are cohorts that have come to age at different points of time in history. The phenomenon is not very different from people growing up around the world in different parts and imbibing certain values defined by their environment. It is to be expected that those born within the same generation will grow up with "collective memories" based on the critical social and cultural events they lived through together, and these will cause them to harbour specific norms, attitudes, and behaviours. A generation will be shaped by a range of social, historical, and technological forces.

It is acceptable to formulate and examine identity-based stereotypes on this frontier. This in turn makes it easy to allow putdowns and prejudice that can cause needless harm. What is needed is a cultural space where generations can respect and learn from each other. None of us after all have any control over what generation we are born into!

As all things human go, the arrival of a new generation, like that of any newcomer to an established order may seem like a threat. Here comes more competition for resources. So, when the precablers feel their experience threatened by the digital savvy of Millennials and Gen Z, they get all defensive and dismiss them as "entitled snowflakes". To any guidance or feedback offered by the precablers and Gen Xers, the young may respond with a shrug and an "OK, Boomer." It's not a comfortable feeling to have the validity of their own view undermined thus.

The goal ought to be to move past such defensive mindsets so that these differences can be turned into an opportunity for collaboration and growth. A greater empathy, cooperation, and trust can lead to a combination of resources to create something mutually beneficial. But what in particular are we struggling to understand about the Millennials and Gen Z?

What in our collective mind, for instance, is the millennial's vulnerable spot? Their famed burnout! Now is it a cover for entitled laziness or is it just plain old common fatigue brought on by a long to-do list? Depending on the view we take, the advice is likely to sound prescriptive. One, stop being so lazy and two, do less, why don't you? The clear presumption is that humans are in complete command of their bodies and minds and it is therefore merely a matter of exercising the right choices. It is inconceivable for a boomer to appreciate that some forces larger than us might be at play around the Millennials.

It has been cited that Millennials are subject to social, technological, and economic pressures that threaten to overwhelm the nervous system and wear out all their coping mechanisms. And therefore, the psychic and physical symptoms associated with burnout: such as anxiety, depression, insomnia, weakened immunities, loss of appetite, and substance abuse as also depleted energy levels. But surely this is not the first generation to suffer from overwork and exhaustion. Has no other cohort in the past had to adapt to new forms of technology and culture? There have in fact, been historical precedents. Theological writings from the late medieval era speak of 'acedia' or a depressive world-weariness that induced lethargy and distraction, preventing true contact with God. Writers from the nineteenth century coined the term 'neurasthenia' for the overburdening of the nervous system caused by the daily onrush of stimuli generated by the new urban industrial society. So then, what has changed for the Millennials?

The burnt-out (or acediac or neurasthenic) self is thoroughly weary of activity but unable to find rest. This is different from simple exhaustion that stems from depleted energy levels that can be restored through sleep. Now compare this "ethereal tiredness" with the anxious weariness described by some Millennials. They feel stalked from within by the assurance that they could do anything they put their minds to. This sentiment is specific to the millennial burnout. The effect of this kind of message is ambiguous. It can spur ambition and achievement, but it can also leave the recipient of it forever feeling as though they're falling short, that they could do more, attain more, and be more. And no, this isn't a message this generation is receiving exclusively from their parents; it is in fact, the maxim of our entire culture, amplified at every moment by the ideals of beauty, accomplishment, talent and taste — perfect homes, bodies, families, jobs — beamed at us from magazine pages, TV screens, and social media feeds. It is an internal persecution of the most insidious kind. The voice that sings we can! Work harder and be better at everything, even rest and recuperation. Achieving our best selves begins to seem like a mirage. There is an ever-present dissatisfaction with who we are and what we have.

And it is our youngest generation that is reading all the headlines mocking their millennial predecessors. It makes them even more determined probably to push back at any age-oriented stereotypes coming their way. Even though they are at the bottom of the pecking order, they have gone on the offensive so as to defend themselves. They launched a pre-emptive strike against the Baby Boomers recently using the most powerful weapons in their arsenal — social messaging platforms such as

TikTok, Snapchat, and Instagram. Their retort to the old-school and out of touch generation was "OK, Boomer."

Don't believe climate change is real? OK, Boomer. Want to call all young people "snowflakes" and blame them for every ill in the world? OkBoomer. The phrase has gone viral, appearing in memes and merchandise being bought up by the Gen Z crowd. Their views of information and communication have been shaped by social media and fake news. The rapid pace of change means Gen Z can be more knowledgeable about technology than people twice as old. This generation has grown up empowered by their parents and their high school peers who have created empires from their smartphones as YouTube stars and Instagram influencers.

The thing is, "None of us is as smart as all of us." OK, Gen Z?

Industry of Guilt

My forefathers tilled the land.

My Dad's father was the first-generation learner and he studied up to "matric", the term in use back then for Class 10. His medium of instruction was Urdu. I remember leafing through his account books in wonder. The letters he wrote us began with the standard and never changing form of address for my father, *"Barkhurdaar Harnek Singh"*. His dream was to see his two sons through the Punjab Agricultural College (now University), Ludhiana.

Papa Ji must have had visions of his sons returning to the soil at the end of their agricultural degrees. My father instead joined the Army Education Corp. As we moved, nomad like, from one cantonment to the other, there remained a constant. We three siblings were placed in the best schools available locally.

But I grew up with an acute sense of the lack of educated units in our family. There was hard work; you saw enterprise, even the smarts of the street but no weighty professional degree in the immediate vicinity. I remember the wondrous amazement I felt, at acquaintances that seemed to have sprung from a lineage of professionals, creative artists, families that had learning as their grammar, their history, their geography.

And soon enough, it was my turn. I had wanted to become a full-fledged journalist. But in the India of the late 70s, anyone who scored decently took up the Science stream in senior school. I did not risk that beaten track even though life gave me my second chance to swing back to my original love in the Vice Principal's office at Fergusson College, Pune in 1980. Dr. Pathak, the Vice Principal was looking at me, pen poised over two check boxes on the admission form: Chemistry or English Literature? I mumbled feebly, "Can I do both?" He shook his head and ticked the box marked Chemistry.

That decision became my personal red flag, a betrayal of the self almost. Little wonder that its aftertaste coagulated over the following years, into a concrete resolve to help my own daughters identify their core interests first. And that is how it came about that an arduous and busy process of raising them to experience a range of fields ended the day we stood at the gates of the National Law School of India University, Bangalore with our firstborn. Round one had clicked!

It is hard to describe the emotions of middle-class Indian parents leading their child into one of the country's premier and coveted schools of learning. There is awe, there is pride, there is gratitude, and most of all, there is a sense of validation, of having done the right by the young. I was like Mrs. Bhamra of Bend it like Beckham, "At least I taught her full Indian dinner, the rest is up to God."

It wasn't long before the talk of graduation date began doing the rounds. The campus placements, however, came and went; our ward did not register for any. "Why deprive someone else who is really keen on a corporate job?" she told us. Ditto for the "Teach for India" platform which glimmered one instant, pausing briefly but only to whizz past. There was a lot of thinking and agonizing and analyzing afoot and more and more, the house was reverberating with two words, "Public Policy".

The futuristic images that had taken shape in our minds over the five years of law school gradually began to dissolve at the edges. It was getting increasingly clear that the beaten track was going to be given the miss this time in my life. We stood by, her father and I, and watched the mental upheaval involved with a mix of concern and pride.

More and more, I was beginning to understand the rationale of the paths most taken. Of course, there is the security of the known, the comfort of crystal-clear directions, and the certainty of cruising home. But what do you say to this, "Mom, I am twenty-two years old. I spent five years at India's best law school. The serve is mine to return. We have to stop fearing failure. At my age and with my degree, if I don't take a risk, who will?"

Even though I have lived my life by the dictum that attitude matters more than facts and that the mind can bring about anything it visualizes strongly enough, I have shuddered at the audacity of the young life planners today. Are they being too wishful and unrealistic? Are they off the mark in agonizing so much over discovering what it is, their heart hankers after? Are they right in trying to cram everything into one lifetime? What are the odds that they will lead their lives with a reasonable measure of happiness with so many conflicting needs? Are they setting themselves up for a lifetime of frustration with their 'instant gratification' theory? Is it them who have it wrong or is it us, with our jaded, apologetic, and fearful tales?!

I can't help but stoop to pick up my jaw every time I stand across a twenty-something, holding forth on the milestones they see very clearly on their life's journey. The predominant sense is of a worldly wisdom far beyond their years. It is as though life has fitted them with far-seeing binoculars that ruthlessly filter out all romance and airy, bubble views.

My response to the fifty-year plans I hear is a mix of admiration, concern and a shade of what they call 'bleh'. Why this heart-breaking awareness; this excessive need for a sense of control and order? While I marvel at their courage to follow their heart, I wonder if there is just that misstep between the plausible and the possible.

Of course, we have a role to play in this 'all or nothing' theme song when we offer unconditional support to our young. It is we who bring them up to think all paths are smooth when we do not allow them to bear the consequences of their actions. Perhaps we spoil them by always standing by. There may even be anxiety born of a relationship so open with parents that everything is shared, including misgivings and insecurities. And with so much generic alarm and mess around them, is it any wonder so many young people suffer from insomnia and depressive disorders.

What an industry of guilt around parenthood we have built up, we dare not be anything but the most appeasing, reassuring, understanding, accepting, deep breathing Moms, and Dads. I now believe there might have been a sense of reassurance, even security in our parents' non-committal ways!

This generation ought to be whooping with joy. They are path-breakers in that no other lot had their brand of educated, supportive, and aware fathers and mothers. They are enviably poised to be able to have their cake, eat it and take some home too!

The Amazeballs

Twenty years ago, when I was busy shunting my girls between the Talkatora Stadium and the Kathak Kendra, New Delhi I wouldn't have known I would be allaying their climate anxiety two decades later, stuck inside a house with them during the lockdown. Time and again, the older of them has urged us to invest in a place far away over the hills. The idea of digging trenches to escape climatic hell is very present and real in her head. But we have the typical inertia of the boomers. I would never have bargained for the social media activism of the teens we are seeing today. They were supposed to be reading Hardy Boys and Nancy Drew series. When did they become so ready to take over the crown from the Millennials? And ready they are.

They are here, all itching to redefine political movements, religion, popular culture, and values. Known as Generation Z—born between 1995 and 2012—they are the world's first truly connected generation but with the mandate of maintaining physical social distancing and they are, at this very moment living to tell the tale of one of the globe's greatest pandemics. Change seems to be a bigger constant in their lives than any other generation gone by. Digital natives, masters at filtering, and inheritors of great economic distress are the Gen Z.

According to a 2019 Bloomberg report, Gen Z makes up for 32 percent of the global population, with India's Gen Z population at 472 million. This generation is described as the counterfoil to the dreamy Millennials. Raised by Gen X, they are seen as being self-reliant. A theory has it that they prefer skills over paycheques, experiences over careers, and have little patience for societal norms or parental approvals. They have already given an account of themselves on the scale of responsibility. In fact, some of them had begun to worry about the COVID-19 even before India had its first case because there was severe anxiety over the country's perceived inability to deal with it.

Isolation. Apocalypse. I have heard these words from my children. One of them has felt caged during the lockdown, not being able to cross interstate borders on drives. But I do believe that in the Zoomers, the Millennials have met more than a match in stubbornness. Here is a generation as bent upon, if not more, on not compromising their aspirations to match the much-touted notions of reality. Their smartphones are their umbilical cords and their Snapchat is chill. For this wired generation, real-world friendships begin with social media profiling. The online world does seem far more significant to them than the physical world and there is none of the older generation's scepticism. They also do not appear to be as smitten by celebrities as those gone before. Their own individuality is important to them.

According to Shiv Visvanathan, eminent social scientist and Director, Centre for the Study of Knowledge Systems, OP Jindal Global University, Gen Z is "part hypothesis, part fiction, part reality". He argues how the generation "has been launched but not quite arrived." He goes on to add, "The core character of this generation is that it was launched like a piece of technology, a part of the innovation chain rather than of a generational cycle. Its appeal is newness, a lack of memory, where there is little or nothing of the burden of history."

Do the Zoomers realize they are a privileged lot? Do they appreciate that some brave Millennials paved the way for their easy participation in Pride Parades? Do they see that it indeed is possible for them to change the world, "one day at a time"? Do they note how unique they are in being the youngest generational breed of writers releasing their novels and books with enviable aplomb?

This is a breed that is well-informed. "They do not accept anything on its face value whether it is religion, culture, or education. A generation, which is focused more on better services than products," says Achal Sharma of Corepeeler Foundation. They are also greatly aware of their environment. Open-minded and willing to correct the mistakes of their previous generations, the climate emergency movement is mostly made up of the younger generation—20-year-olds that are willing to make changes in their lifestyles. They, after all, have had to learn and discover a whole lot all by themselves.

According to the latest UN figures, India is home to the world's largest youth population. Almost 600 million are below the age of 25, which is half of the country's population. Of India's 1.3 billion population, 27 percent is between the age of 10–24 years which roughly translates to the country's Gen Z population. They are growing up in a participative economy. Technology has democratized their existence and replaced the silver spoon with the idea of a tech fork. More solo in temperament than the Millennials, the Zoomers are entrepreneurial, multitasking, and pragmatic. And what they are looking for is flexibility, openness, and meaningfulness in the kind of work they're being assigned. It is no longer just about survival or work-life balance; it is more about making meaningful contributions in their roles.

Youthfully arrogant and a trifle impatient, the Zoomers will want to rule the world on their own terms. Rational far more than religious, they are at ease with relationships and happy to participate in dialogues. Does peer pressure look like becoming redundant? Unbelievable. Self-expression, co-living, and coworking come naturally to them. Their fundamental belief in co-existing is what makes them co-creators for the brands.

But conversations around Gen Z are not yet psychologized and still need to be given a perspective, a history, and a profile. "For now, it has no biography, everything about it is conjecture. It still has to be sociologized," says Visvanathan, and cites how this generation has no role models or exemplars and is waiting to invent itself. "It is the emptiest of the literary fiction created. It needs to grow. It is the future that has to unfold as biography," he adds.

Dua Lipa's song sure sits easy on them, "Walk away, you know how… Don't start caring about me now."

The Matchmaker

Have you driven past a movie hall stealing surreptitious glances at the bold billboard? *'Gupt gyan'*, it declares, almost like a dare. You must have been one short of your teen years back then. There was this hush hush air about the movie. Those were erotically challenged times in retrospect. A lot under the carpet, more behind open umbrellas and the rest within the four walls. Hearts stayed where they belonged, in the thoracic cavity.

Godfather, Lolita, and the odd Playboy magazine comprised the entire spectrum of sex education for the Baby Boomers. Mandakini in *Ram Teri Ganga Maili* and Zeenat Aman in *Satyam Shivam Sundaram* would have seared many a triggered mind. Reams were written on the bold scenes of Rehana Sultan in films like *Chetna* and *Dastak*. And who can forget Lakshmi as the lush Julie against Vikram as the fervid Shashi Bhattacharya. Then comes Bobby in her ascendent dress and dewdrop face. Those were the *"gapoochi gapoochi gum gum"* days. So much was *"Khel Khel Mein"*. It took a simple finger on a fainting woman's pulse to confirm pregnancy. Shame shrouded both private and public life like New Delhi's asphyxiating pollution.

The unutterably gruesome word people only hissed in asides to describe a relationship was "affair". You could never be in one, you had to have had an affair. And it was red in colour! Boys and girls in co-ed schools were the fifth and sixth castes. They barely spoke to each other. The only acceptable social connection between the two genders was that of siblings. You were either brother and sister or husband and wife. Mainstream genders were only two in number.

Who would have known of the pleasure fest waiting to break upon the subcontinent? And with such an array of arrangements. You could hang out, hook up, or be into. You could be breadcrumbing, peacocking or micro cheating. You could be in a relationship or a talkship or a situationship. Mono, bi, or poly? Decision paralysis or a healthy compromise? Just like a cereal shopper in the Big Bazaar!

Marriage? What a slow down! Life is to be lived lightly and in tiny instalments. Who wants to bear the burden of eventual in-laws, eventual children, eventual grief? Young people today believe in giving each other plenty of space, they have no plans of taking over each other's lives. It's a common tale, mom throws away her career for the family, children grow up watching their parents' joyless marriage, more a habit than a choice. Why would women settle for something as insipid, they do not need men to support them?

But how do unmarried couples find apartments to rent, given how allergic landlords are even to the singles. Don't the busybody realtors advise them to get married? How do living-in pairs deal with their nosy families? How do their friends react? How does society view the man and the woman involved? Equally accountable? Chances are that the woman gets whispered about as a slut because she smokes in the balcony and the man is regarded as a bystander, a victim even.

In time though, more and more, the community comes to accept these arrangements. Neighbourly exchanges and festive gifts take care of the bristling moral umbrage. Do the parents know? Don't ask, don't tell is probably the formula. And no, living together is certainly not the norm but it's common enough for laws to be changed. It was in early 2010 that the Supreme Court legalized live-in relationships in India. The apex court stated that if two sound-minded adults of the opposite sex wanted to live together without getting married, it was not a crime. This verdict was reached in response to twenty-two charges of criminal offense filed in 2005 against actress Khushboo after her statement to magazines supporting live-in relationships and premarital sex in India. The Supreme Court further stated that a live-in relationship qualified as a 'relationship in the nature of marriage', if four requirements are met. First, the couple must hold themselves out to society as being akin to spouses. Second, they must be of legal age to marry. Third, they must be qualified to enter into a legal marriage, and fourth they must have voluntarily cohabited for a significant period of time. Such a relationship would come under the jurisdiction of the Protection of Women from Domestic Violence Act, and the Hindu Marriage Act of 1976 would allow children from such a relationship to be legitimate, establishing succession and property rights.

The older generations do not see any sense in live-in relationships. In fact, there was a time when even after two people were engaged, they were discouraged from meeting too often because intimacy apparently creates contempt. Is it that there is the fear of the partners learning about each other's deficiencies and then choosing to opt-out? There is also the issue of the woman's chastity. Live-in relationships bring the worst fear of the older generations to life. But the Millennials and Zoomers are questioning the views of their parents. They watch television shows like *Friends*, and they wonder how they can possibly spend the rest of their lives with someone without a thorough understanding of their habits and their angularities. The age-old formula of marry first and then love will follow is being questioned as people become keenly interested in romance, love, self-discovery, and exploration. There is greater scope today for being experimental. There is also a new notion of marriage as a personal domain, rather than a cultural or familial one.

We, the middle class have had a change of morality of sorts. Women have relative economic independence and as more and more young people move away from home to study and work there are greater opportunities for experimenting with relationships other than marriage. India is changing at a break-neck pace; it is a constant yo-yo between the past and the present, between the East and the West, between the glittery new images on TV and the dusty, outdated ones of the earlier generations.

Here they come

"Ma, I don't want to pursue law after my law school is over, my passion is elsewhere. I am not sure where but I will figure it out."

"Pa, I don't have the bandwidth for news that so reflects the state's stupidity!"

"I don't care about investing in houses and cars; this does not wash in the environment we live in today."

"Why is the family not reserving space in the hills or digging trenches, what is our climate crisis backup?"

"Marriage is such a patriarchal institution; it doesn't make sense anymore."

"Why would I let society or family decide what my identity ought to be?"

"You only live once; I don't want to miss out on anything."

"All that matters is authenticity, I have to be true to myself."

These millennial statements were flying in the air barely five years ago and they still are. Breakup parties, school graduation continuation parties, parents out-of-town parties, bachelorette binges, hookah lounges, the gay pride parade, the kinky collective, queer dating apps, vegans, vipassana attendees, kheerganga trekkers, hash-tag Himachal…my 80 plus mother would say, "We'll see how long their *jawani* lasts!!"

Well, Moms are usually right because lo and behold, the new youth is here. And what are our Zoomers saying? Why, about the Millennials of course!

"They are past their expiry dates, no big ideas there."

"They are not very good with hashtags and gifs."

"What is this obsession with small and simple things? So excited about growing a beetroot!"

"When will they outgrow Harry Potter's Butterbeer recipes?"

"These guys are in denial, posting filtered pictures of their coffee on Instagram, we don't use glitter, we are real."

"We're a lot more political than they were at our age."

"We are desensitized; they seem to have internalized the snowflakiness and are sensitive."

"Nothing is really off-limits for us because everything bad that could have happened has already happened."

Alright, so Millennials have had it rough at the hands of boomers but now it is Gen Z coming for them. The wheel is clearly turning if only partially. Because unlike my generation, Millennials do seem to show support for the concerns of Gen Z. They seem to, in fact, go a bit overboard with lauding their ideas and outspokenness. Oh no, they don't dismiss them as greenhorns, they, in fact, listen to the Zoomers. It's another matter that Zoomers consider the millennial TikToks lame and in time may even come to resent their burdening them with saving the dying planet.

There is more. A difference in the degree of their generational sense of humour, the Zoomers claiming superiority here since they consider themselves more desensitized. A few weeks ago, there was this serial killer on the run, a double murder suspect called Peter Manfredonia. Gen Zs decided to invade his social media pages and comment with emojis. They flooded him with really weird, overtly happy comments to try making fun of him. While Manfredonia's family publicly asked for him to turn himself in, his since-removed Instagram profile was overrun with comments poking fun at and making light of the murders he's accused of. And do they find episodes of *"Friends"* equally funny, if the Zoomers watch those at all! There may also be a view of what is perceived as the millennial habit of oversharing their personal experiences.

In recent years marketers have harboured a common misconception that Gen Z and Millennials are essentially the same. It is true that they are both highly connected to technology and the internet and can be considered to fit the category of "young adults" but while one is on their Finsta and TikTok, the other is still on Facebook. There is also a huge age difference, with the oldest Millennials being close to 40 and the youngest members of Gen Z still in second grade.

Millennials grew up using DVD players, giant personal computers, cell phones with tiny screens, and dial-up internet. At that time, we thought these technologies were groundbreaking. Now, most children and teens within Gen Z have access to iPads, smartphones, endless Wi-Fi, or streaming services that put our prized DVD players to shame. While Millennials watched innovation begin, Gen Z was immersed in it from day one. And this has taken a toll. As per research, Gen Z is a socially conscious generation but also the loneliest, with far more body image, mental health, and cyberbullying issues than any other age group in the past.

And while both the generations care about finances and are known for improving on the financial habits of past generations, Millennials put their money into buying more products or services that will give them a positive experience, while Gen Z is more focused on savings and practical products. Although both spend a lot of time on the internet, while Millennials spend around 7.5 hours online, Gen Z surfs for nearly 10 hours. They both go online primarily with mobile devices. Gen Z's mobile-first mindset also impacts how they shop. Members of this generation are twice as likely to make a mobile online purchase than Millennials. When it comes to online content consumption, both Millennials and Gen Z spend most of their time watching videos and visiting social media sites, but the platforms they use are quite different. While Millennials thrived on Facebook, Instagram, LinkedIn, and Twitter, Gen Z seems happy using video-based platforms like Instagram, YouTube, Snapchat, and TikTok. The two social platforms in common are Instagram and YouTube, pulling in both Millennials and the video-loving Gen Z members. YouTube is also the second-most used search engine and a platform where many in Gen Z and millennial generations go for product research.

When it comes to content consumption, each generation's habits align well with its average attention span. While Millennials are known to pay attention to content for twelve seconds, Gen Z will only stay focused on it for eight seconds. Furthermore, Gen Z enjoys quick or short-form video content, like that of Snapchat or Instagram Stories, while Millennials value long-form content, such as detailed videos or podcasts.

Gen Z wants to focus on content that feels more informative and less like an ad. In fact, 84% of Gen Z will skip video ads as quickly as possible while 65% of them have downloaded some type of ad-blocker on their mobile devices or computers.

According to various studies, Gen Z members expect added service from a brand when they make purchases. They also value free delivery and discounts or coupons. And although Millennials may come out as more frivolous buyers, they also earn more annually than most older generations, they are the most educated age group, and are notably optimistic about their futures.

While both Millennials and Gen Z are driven by higher education and career growth, Gen Z adults are more financially motivated than the millennial generation. Gen Z also applies for jobs more aggressively than past generations. It is the Gen Z that is expected to be more driven to make and save money. It is the practicality of a product over the "trendiness" of it for them, always and every time.

The Moral Code

How do generations reason about moral problems? Do the Millennials exhibit differences in moral reasoning and what are those based upon? What have the trends been in moral reasoning over time?

Most boomers and Gen Xers will likely say that right and wrong do not change ever. But far more Millennials and Zoomers seem to have a more fluid view of what is right and what is wrong. They do seem to harbour some form of content bias based on factors such as business interests, gender, intelligence, work experience, and the context or the pull of the story. It does appear that ideas on morality are no longer as stable as they were once. They are in fact, relative today. Every generation alive is not on the same page on morality and this has not been debated or reckoned with.

Is there truly a decline in moral behaviour and are we concerned? Could moral behaviour possibly be legislated? Implement laws, in other words, to encourage people to act in moral ways? Were there ever any laws on moral standards? Have some been removed? How do humans make moral judgements? How do they decide between right and wrong on a personal level? What factors weigh into these decisions? Perhaps some want to consider whether or not someone is getting hurt in determining if something is right or wrong. They might want to know whether something is legal or whether the benefits outweigh the costs when thinking about morality. There may be worries about what the majority of people think or whether an institution gets hurt or whether there is bound to be some embarrassment and loss of face. Some form of a moral compass is at play and it is influenced by faith, geography, education, and gender.

What generally are the factors that shape the shared moral views of a society? Parents, religious beliefs, feelings, friends, teachers, and the media? Is there any one influential source of morality that is embraced by the majority? According to research from Business Ethics Professor Dr. James Weber, Executive Director of the Institute for Ethics in Business at Duquesne University, when compared to past generations, Millennials exhibit lower levels of cognitive moral reasoning. In research he conducted with Ethics and Business Law Professor Dr. Dawn R. Elm at the University of St. Thomas, Weber compared Millennials' levels of cognitive moral reasoning to secondary analysis from other studies on the moral reasoning demonstrated by Baby Boomers and Generation Xers when these generations were in college in the 1960s and 1970s and the 1980s and 1990s, respectively. The studies showed that Baby Boomers used principled moral reasoning (the highest level of decision-making) about 42% of the time and Generation Xers on average used principled moral reasoning 37% of the time. Millennials only used principled moral reasoning 31% of the time.

When asked what prompted this specific research, Weber said it was because Millennials increasingly are a growing influence in the workforce, marketplace, and investment environment. "They are a force to be reckoned with, given their unique ideals, beliefs, and practices, which prompted us to begin our exploration to better understand Millennials' cognitive moral reasoning," he said.

Life as a millennial executive is replete with having to make decisions that have moral or ethical dimensions. It can catch one off guard. You see a colleague being mistreated by your boss—do you speak up? You don't agree with a decision that comes down from senior management—how do you explain it to your subordinates? When pushed, most would admit that they rely on their inner moral code to take a call. But how nuanced is this moral code? Organizations don't often provide opportunities to develop a finer understanding of moral challenges. In fact, there hardly is any moral debate. Self-preservation is likely to weigh in on verdicts too.

For 20 years, Harvard Business School's literature class 'The Moral Leader' has been teaching a literature-based leadership. Through the close study of novels, plays, and historical accounts—followed by deep classroom discussion, this innovative course encourages students to confront fundamental moral challenges, to develop skills in moral analysis and judgment, and to come to terms with their own definition of moral leadership. The course taps into a rich collection of fiction and nonfiction to offer executives enduring lessons on leadership.

The value of 'The Moral Leader' is said to be not so much in what the instructors have to say during the course but in how the students reason through the moral challenges together and debate the perspectives that the literature evokes. Here is a tool that can be used to spark revealing conversations that do not get an opportunity to happen anywhere other than a person's own echo chamber.

The exercise enables business executives to distance themselves from their prejudices and later, upon reflection, see how their own decisions compare with those in the stories. Consider Kazuo Ishiguro's novel, *The Remains of the Day*, about an English butler who reflects on a life devoted to a single moral principle: loyalty to his boss. The sacrifice this demands of him has some terrifying consequences for himself and those around him. It is the story of a moral code taken to extremes. There is a cautionary tale there about the limits of loyalty and the points at which we start to lose ourselves to our jobs.

The Remains of the Day would make for a great solitary read, but if you were to wrestle with your own moral code, you would need to debate the point with others and sift several views. Such an exchange of ideas can give people an appreciation of how their own moral codes constrain them and how they might approach decisions with a more layered understanding. Most of us believe that our moral beliefs are self-evident. But hearing points of view you had never thought of is one way to strengthen your own moral reasoning skills and arrive at a great depth of an intergenerational insight.

Interestingly there is an 'Outline for the Implementation of Citizen Moral Construction in the New Era' across the Galwan valley. There is 'advice' on how to raise children, surf the internet and behave while abroad, almost a life guide for the inhabitants of what shall be the 'middle kingdom' between Heaven and Earth. If only "The Moral Leader" were a course mandated for world leaders, those leading powerhouses in particular.

As good as our stories

"What we deplore is not that the gate of western knowledge was thrown open to Indians, but that such knowledge was imported to India at the sacrifice of our own cultural heritage. What was needed was a proper synthesis between the two systems and not neglect, far less destruction, of the Indian base," Syama Prasad Mukherjee

India has the 6th largest number of World Heritage Sites in the world, 38 in number. There are 30 cultural sites, 7 natural sites, and 1 mixed as recognized by UNESCO.

If you were to stop the average John, Jaani, Janardhan on the road with this story he would shrug it off! In a country struggling under the crushing weight of poverty, illiteracy, and corruption, any mention of heritage is treated with incredulity, "People are dying here and you are talking about preserving history!" Oh no, we are not a nation too high on heritage walks or recording of ruins! The appreciation of glorious history is a luxury, as far as we see it, befitting races that are developed beyond the basic sustenance mark. Those are people who have sublimed beyond survival, with refined antennae for finer levels of cultural assimilation. We are too caught up meanwhile to be watching the back door out of which, unknown to us, our history and heritage are quietly vanishing.

A far greater number of people study Sanskrit outside of India today, for one. Hindustani music and classical dances have more and more takers outside the country. The most authoritative and best-researched books on our history, our culture, and our socio-religious nuances are written by non-Indians. We are oblivious, indifferent, and dismissive of our phenomenal legacy. If pushed, most Indians will claim a sense of pride in what is known as the "5000-year continuous civilization" but scratch some more, and the shocking fault lines will show up.

In a typical Indian home, any talk of the hoary past is synonymous with excavating buried ghosts and likely to invite impatience! There is little sense of lineage or history inculcated in the children. Most learn from watching their family elders who do not respect or recall family lore. The contempt for what has gone before extends into schools and colleges where History and Sociology are trashed as subjects inferior to the analytical Sciences and requiring only rote memory at that. There is nil acknowledgment of the urgent need to infect the new generations with the desire to claim, take charge of, and guard their own historical narrative.

We forget that we are only as good as our stories. And to grow unscathed beyond our diversity, we have to come to grips with our past, outlined in our own idiom. To move forward with vigour and conviction, we need to constantly look back at our common cultural wealth. Those are our survival coordinates. It will give us strength and lasting power to know and interpret our monuments, our sites, our deities, our traditions, our beliefs ourselves rather than have others tell us what we are about.

How wretched must our children feel on foreign campuses, to meet others who perhaps knew more about their history and heritage than they did? How did our records come to be in such a terrible state of disrepair? It is no secret that we hang clotheslines on archive balconies and house our historical treasures in rooms with broken windows and leaky roofs. Pigeon poop on priceless papers is not unusual and the less said about the ill-trained and destructive staff, the better. Arguably, of the 1000 plus heritage structures in Delhi alone, many are soot-covered on the inside from the squatters' *chullah* smoke!

One does not hear any talk of the crisis need to preserve our heritage sites on any popular and mass forum. The deplorable fact is that there is no domestic labouring or analysing or applying or studying our past. The Indian National Trust for Art and Cultural Heritage (INTACH) is forever looking for Heritage Walk Leaders to lead their weekend meanders.

I have been on some of their walks with Jaya Basera, Heritage Consultant, and passionate advocate for heritage conservation. The average size of the group she leads is about ten in all, an atom of the ocean that is Delhi! But the stories she relates and the facts she quotes, bring to life an achingly beautiful echo from the days done. Hidden under the dust and grime and foliage are sounds, sights, and smells of a bygone era, a foundation on which we stand today. Ironically, India's conservation quick fix for all these hauntingly charming monuments is to put a lock at the entrance and keep out the intrepid urinators, dogs, romancing couples, and future cricketers.

Besides funding and expertise for the regular upkeep of heritage properties, the authorities have been struggling to create awareness and a sense of belonging among citizens regarding architectural wealth. Vandalism and defacement are two big challenges that neutralize most conservation efforts. Perhaps we do not cultivate a concern in our Zoomers about where we have come from? We are too caught up in the mundane grind to hear historic notes straining to reach us from our crumbling glory? What is the state of our common legacy? In what condition does our combined heritage exist? Noted author and historian Swapna Liddle says, "Though these projects need refinement and not just footfalls, the communities must work in partnership with experts and private parties, where heritage can be a great engine for development. Until we, as stakeholders, take interest and responsibility, preservation is not possible." The experts are unanimous that unless conservation is liberalized, we have no future, and corporates and civil society need to be equal partners.

It costs just fifty bucks to take our kids on one of the heritage walks and sow the seed that might one day fill this void in our national portrait. The truth is that if you were to take away from us our history, literature, culture, we would cease to exist!

The Koreaboos

Parenting is a crowded vocation today, what with the internet and peers vying with Papa and Mama for the child's growth and development.

I was talking to a dear friend two days ago. "How is Junior doing?" is a query bound to come up fairly early in the exchange. I remember listening to the update on Junior's growing fascination with K- Pop. The eleven-year-old was hatching plans to go to South Korea and join the Super Junior boy band, the male version of Girls' Generation that is a YouTube sensation, with their song "Gee" having passed 47 million views. Junior was largely home during this remote schooling phase and was spending hours poring over the modalities of becoming the hottest act in pop music. He had begun to take Korean language instruction online and had chalked up a career map for himself. It had bullet points on where he would stay in Seoul, what part-time jobs he would be doing to support himself during the auditioning period, and the career switches he would make after 26 years since that was the average longevity of an artist.

While Ma and Pa worked their regimented jobs in the service of the nation, Junior sat at home fantasizing about colouring his hair lavender and bedazzling his eyes with rhinestone makeup. I listened to the bemused and half-proud note in the parent's voice over the phone. She was clearly not taking this preoccupation too seriously. It was being dismissed as a childish fantasy that was sure to resolve into a regular career plan as time lapsed but I was not so certain. To my tentative note of caution, the response was, "Ma'am, I have given him full freedom, whatever he wants to do!"

In retrospect, I am not so sure just this large-hearted, good faith benevolence is enough. It is important today to foresee and anticipate the twists and turns that are sure to come up ahead from the upbringing that the www and peers are providing one other. In this instance, for example, is enough thought being given to Junior's game plan? Have some all-important questions been voiced? Will Junior feel comfortable and be included in the unfamiliar Korean culture? Has the stress of "being different" been factored in? Do we know the inside mechanics of this international rage called K-Pop? What does the competition look like? What are the cultural values you will be up against? How well can you expect to fit in? And should you not make the cut, what is the coping strategy going to be like?

I have done this. I sent my 17-year-old off to Princeton University pleasantly lulled into thinking that a scholarship, international ranking and a progressive school brochure was sound enough insurance against aloneness and a theoretical assimilation. In any case, who says no to Princeton University? I was starry-eyed at the thought of my child on a campus that Albert Einstein and John Nash roamed once. Imagine my surprise when I learnt that although diversity was upheld as a stated value, the practice of it was squeamish. There is an inbuilt tentativeness to being a small brown Asian amid the tall Americans of European descent, the low-grade adrenal fatigue of being an outsider.

The thing called 'exposure' that my generation and the one gone before used to take great pride in providing and possessing. You can no longer be very sure of the nature and intent of that engagement anymore. Take for example, Girls' Generation, this tandem of nine young pop singers and dancers that has become an intercontinental rage. Their fans hold flashmobs in cities like Paris and Los Angeles, demanding that concerts be held there. A company like Samsung is riding the band's coattails to market their products in several countries. But it's not the music itself that is causing the sensation; it's how the groups are using marketing and cultural outreach to gain attention.

How does Junior or his parents know that he is not at the receiving end of a well-crafted "Culture Technology (CT)" approach to designing and seeding Korean pop culture in foreign markets to expand their global appeal? A concept developed by Lee Soo Man, founder of SM Entertainment, the largest talent agency in South Korea, SM Entertainment and other similar talent agencies have a contractual relationship with their stars and control of their private lives. There are hundreds of young talents on their rolls who are trained to sing, dance, act, and speak foreign languages. A strategy is in place to embed more and more foreign singers from strategic markets into larger girl or boy bands. These imported singers are then used to promote their acts back in their respective home countries.

It was in July 2016, that the mega-hit "Gangnam Style" by South Korean singer PSY surpassed 2.6 billion views on YouTube. Big Bang, a Korean pop (K-Pop) boy band, earned $44 million in 2015, making it among the highest paid in the industry. The global success of K-Pop has not happened by accident. It took strategic talent management, customer relationships built via social media, and localized product offerings.

One is unsure if Junior realizes that SM Entertainment hosts annual auditions in several countries, from the U.S. to Kazakhstan, and selects a few trainable and marketable individuals out of more than 300,000 applicants. Their training then is like boot camp. The trainees live in dorms, practice 12 hours a day and are given lessons in singing, dancing, and acting in addition to foreign languages. Every time a trainee performs a song, it's got to be perfect. And there are no guarantees they will ever make their professional debut.

Not just Junior, India is a nation in the grip of Hallyu or the "Flow of Korea". The K-craze has caught up with Millennials all over the country, who can't get enough of South Korean music, shows, beauty products, language or food. As his alarm goes off at 6 am, Junior starts his day listening to his favourite K-Pop song—"Fire" by BTS. In fact, his playlist is filled with K-Pop numbers and the walls of his room plastered with posters of all his favourite South Korean TV stars. He and several of his generation call themselves the 'Koreaboos'—a word used to describe persons who are overly obsessed with Korean culture. Junior ought not to be the only one!

The Critical Prevention

Just like sex and sexual identity, sexual assault ought to be an open topic of discussion with the younger generations, never a taboo. Our boys and girls deserve way more than we are doing. To start with, we can be rest assured that the Zoomers are fairly aware of the cultural movement and messages on sexual assault in the airwaves over the past few years.

The unfortunate truth is that our children are keenly aware of the nature and pervasiveness of sexual assault in our culture. We should have begun discussing it openly with them along with sex and sexual identity a long time ago. Even though not only girls but also boys and young men are sexually assaulted, the perpetrator is invariably a boy or a man. At the core is the idea of consent. This discussion around what constitutes consent ought to be followed by a game plan to face reality. What should a young person do should they ever fall into a situation that feels unsafe or compromising? And can they come to us, to you and me, in the wake of sexual assault?

But is it enough to simply begin talking and practicing prevention? There has to be the talk of consent, respect, and behaviour of course, but it is crucial also to gauge what teenage boys think about the cause and effect of assault. Do they know what the boundaries are? Do they understand what defines sexual assault? Do they appreciate its impact on the victim? Do they have suggestions on how to prevent it?

With new definitions of sexuality and masculinity, there is a sense of insecurity, shame, and confusion amongst many boys. Movements such as those of women empowerment and #MeToo have blurred the notions of what it is to be male in these times. There is a lot out there in the public domain about 'toxic masculinity' but who is outlining 'positive masculinity'?

It is a common misconception that assault is about sex. It is not. It is about power, conquest, and proving oneself a "man". Often these unwelcome actions are prompted by a sense of self-loathing. It is time we begin speaking of maleness in terms of kindness, self-reliance, and respect for women, courage, and a sense of humour. The current discourse about men being a blight on the culture or predators whose dark and damaging impulses need to be reined in is dangerous and utterly self-defeating.

As a society, we have a lot to answer for. The disturbing and heart-rending news stories are an indictment of the blinkers we refuse to take off. It is a comment on our delusional inertia that prevents us from keeping pace with our growing children. The onus is on us adults to stay on top of trends and technology. It is no longer enough to provide for their basic needs, the demand is from us to be their guides and allies and safe spaces.

We could take a few steps right off with reference to sexual assault. The first thing to do would be to stay mindful of our own language and attitudes towards gender stereotypes at home. The next wise step would be to take the mystery out of 'taboo topics' by making them a part of the family's regular conversation at home. For this, parents and educators themselves need to be well-informed and current with the prevailing trends and attitudes. The third thing to do is to literally get into the trenches with the young. 'I don't need to know' is not an option anymore. It would strengthen the mutual connection if parents made an effort to engage with the music and the online content their children are consuming. The young need to know that their parents are plugged into the modern ecosystem. It is as important not to operate from a place of fear and anxiety as it is to not make harsh judgments on the perceived poor choices of our children. The very nature of society and their environment has changed. It is not as linear and programmed as it was when we were teenagers. The final measure would be to throw open your home and heart to their friends irrespective of our opinion of them. When the chips are down, it boils down to open channels of communication.

The open ongoing discussion will most certainly help prevention. It is also bound to keep the idea of consent uppermost for everyone. Such talks with parents and coaches can be extremely powerful. They can change the course of silent suffering for many people. They are bound to affect the attitudes of young people towards the well-being of each other. A shift may likely take place in power dynamics, fear-based thinking, and toxic, externalized self-loathing.

A lot many Zoomers know sexual assault is happening but they don't know what to do. In fact, some may not even be sure they have not committed sexual assault in the past. They often don't know where the lines are drawn. This really is the time for those conversations. Our young need information and tools to help them achieve a wide and lasting cultural change. They will benefit enormously from knowing that the characteristics of positive masculinity include kindness, self-reliance, respect for women, courage, and a sense of humour.

This is our opportunity to help prevent sexual violence. We cannot afford not to use it and use it well. This generation is poised to carry a very different mantle. Even though we are leaving them a harsher world it is they who are forward-thinking and have the potential to develop a deeper sense of humanity.

The idea of the "conquest" of women and boasting of the number they have hooked up with no longer appeals to many young boys for instance. The cultural spiel about and sanction of a male's raging hormones does not wash anymore. We need to acknowledge and support these notions as much as allay the fear and anxiety in potential victims. A phenomenal personal and cultural shift hangs in the balance. Precious young lives are at stake.

The Covid Feminism

At the core of how we conducted the business of living our lives until recently was the assumption that humans existed primarily for each other. There was no cultural recognition of individual autonomy and accountability for developing one's own potential in our tradition. Salvation was spoken of mostly in relation to masculine seekers of truth. The women had either not bothered or had been content to be a 'Mata' or a 'Devi' with supplementary and augmentative functions. One has not heard of a folk thread of a woman needing to or deserving to validate her personal evolution as a better, larger, wiser human being.

And just as women's freedom from the domestic sphere, freedom from financial dependence on men and freedom to access public life was beginning to congeal and be accepted as a matter of course along came the pandemic to undo years of feminist gains. We don't yet know what life will look like in the aftermath but more and more it seems likely that women will be retreating to the one place it has taken them decades to escape from.

That's right. The economy is shrinking. There are huge fears about public health. Public services are in a state of survival mode. It stands to reason therefore that maintenance and care-giving responsibilities will fall upon the home and its maker. Even when the lockdowns lift shyly, not all our needs will be met outside any time soon. These negotiations will be orchestrated by the women primarily. With schools and day-cares closed, responsibilities like childcare and eldercare have become the monopoly of home. Have women's lives in the pandemic;

become more burdened, smaller, and less free? It is true that every single person has a public health obligation to stay home, but only women appear to have a socially enforced responsibility to take on disproportionate domestic work while they are there.

What are the men doing at home, one would ask? As per research, men are in the habit of underestimating the time women have to spend on housework, childcare, and eldercare. It also comes naturally to them to overestimate their own contributions. Who is spending more time home-schooling for one? Now, this looks like becoming a norm in the foreseeable future, with all the plans afoot to implement technology to enable more distanced learning. But if the classroom model is nearing extinction, who will be supervising the kids? Parents? Or Moms? It looks like mothers are well on the way to becoming untrained and unpaid teachers, required to stay home with the children. When schools do reopen, many may use partly remote schedules, with students learning from home for part of the week.

What had once been done away with as a cultural and marital injustice is on the way to becoming a public policy tenet. What happens to the state's obligation to provide an education for children and the associated childcare that it represents? Women will be doing the compensating; it is becoming increasingly clear.

The economic recession caused by the pandemic has disproportionately hit the women-heavy service industries. It is possible that the greater percentages of the newly unemployed are women. Even for those who still have jobs and are working remotely, there is no saying if they will return to the office. Many companies have re-evaluated their overhead costs only to cut down on office space. Some have already announced plans to shift to more permanent work-from-home arrangements after the pandemic. Taken long-term, female productivity is bound to suffer from all the distractions of children, house-work, and domestic disturbances; will this not make them more dispensable to their employers?

The post-pandemic world may mean smaller, more claustrophobic, and more hemmed in lives for women. It could mean women out of work and unable to earn the money that would allow them to provide for their families or gain independence in abusive marriages. Are we heading back to predominantly male realms in public and commerce? Do women seem all set to be the last resort when employers, institutions and the state throw up their hands? This responsibility is sure to translate into lesser freedom and more work.

She used to be primarily a great Mom, keeping a tight check on the kitchen, staying just so in his shadow. He worked hard to provide for the unit, a loyal husband, and an indulgent father. A perfect family portrait but for one latent difference; his portfolio stemmed from himself and hers from those around her. He would be the centre of his own universe; the world around her being the axis she circumvented. His self-esteem came from his personal capability and application in the arena outside the home, her sense of self-worth depended upon approval from those she happened to be related to. He was the doer, she, the pleaser. He had expectations, for her were mostly the adjustments. Marriage embellished the life he already led; it transformed her existence beyond recognition, shifting the very centre of her gravity with a fundamental change in the reason of her being.

And no, neither of them was the villain. They were products of a self-perpetuating social order that was so deep and time tested, it was taken as the given. Yes, there were major shifts in gender-based roles but the foundation stood, only the sheen had dulled and very nervously, at that. Well, guess what, we are coming round a full circle, thank your tiny virus. Women had come a long way. We lived in hope of the day they would begin to stop feeling apologetic for their existence. The world would be a cleaner, more transparent, wholesome, and happier place when it finally began to give women permission and acceptance for self-realization. After all, they were holding up half the sky, or so we believed.

Her middle name is back to being "adjustment". The walking on eggshells and biting the tongue is in place too. Food, shelter, clothing, and security will be seen as compensating enough for a lifetime's devotion to one man and his family. The children better not go off track, which would really be seen as her fault in the final reckoning.

Hold on, the sky seems to be coming down all over again.

Mothers across the generations

Have you met anyone socially and not asked them what their children do? Our culture tells us that the kids are our most visible validation. Their success and failure are ours. Our primary duty is to them, until our last breath. Anything we do for ourselves has to come after their needs have been met. It is fairly common to base retirement plans on the needs of our children. We want to continue to be available to them long past a reasonable expectation and even desire, in some cases.

There is active myopia amongst Indian parents in particular that will not permit them to see that their progeny may be crying for space and independence and liberty. Freedom to be average. To live life from a backpack. To roam the world. To not shoulder family baggage. To just be, for heaven's sake. To shake off the suffocating stranglehold of religion. To run from the forced socializing with extended family. To be released of expectations. To not have to plan, project, invest, save. To not be knocked down by a mace called marriage. To not bring kids into this world and treat them to the uninformed parenting they were themselves subjected to. To earn just enough. To not repay house and car loans. To not lose steam in the rat race. To not have to worry about standing out. To shun brilliance for contentment. To reject competition for an inclusive mediocrity. To listen only to the music of their own hearts. To drop the mask and be themselves. To be able to scream, abuse, love, and experiment. To take risks.

What's wrong with that? You grew up in an age of meagre means. They have matured being waited upon by proud parents and grandparents, their primary enablers that psychology pundits deride today. Don't cry now. You enabled the magnificent Millennial. Gen Z and Gen Alpha to follow!

My grandmother was another story altogether, she lived by one abiding dictum, "Daughters must never be left alone anywhere, overnight." She was obsessive about Mom's friends and rationed her rare friendly visits to the last minute. In fact, she is known to have chucked a pair of scissors at her once, over a five minutes delay, returning home from a class mate's residence, no less. My mother was chaperoned, supervised, guarded, and watched over closely. She did not dare incur my grandmother's wrath.

By the time I came around, the rules had bent more than a bit. I did stay over at one odd home of a colleague for an all-night movie session; there was even a group detour to 'Ghungroo' at the Maurya Sheraton, not leaving the bike ride to Mathura. I went out on school trips, as also outings to do with work. The peripherals had transformed but the core of parental approval still remained intact. Their sanction had to be sought for every little adventure and their happiness was personally important to us.

The tyrannical power of my grandma's generation had given way to a watered-down and benevolent form of authority, a progressive model of parenting tempered with caution. There were no diktats but Dad and Mom's involvement and active presence were presumed. The heavily authoritative tone of the earlier generation had made room for a moderate, accommodating acceptance based on the premise of the parent holding the superior position.

Though we picked careers of our choices and married people mutually chosen for us, we led our lives with our parents as our lodestars. They were there with us, in all of our life's events and it was important to keep them informed, connected, and supportive.

It is 2020 now and two and a half lifetimes later. Children leave home early for college. There is a sense of independence, in personal goals, and life's markers. Many of their emotional needs are met by those outside of the immediate family. Parental approval may still be critical for some but there are likely a few riders. Home is a neater, more convenient hostel. Involvement with household affairs is negligible. They don't necessarily align with the family rhythm. Existing in the twilight zone of digital overload and emotional tentativeness, they inhabit rooms with the 'do not disturb' sign on the doors.

There is a new parent-child vocabulary at play. A parent's affectionate concern could be construed as criticism. Beware of making that friendly but unannounced trip to their place of work. It may come across as interference. Gentle nudges towards life's great truths may be taken as attempts to sabotage their life's passion. The slightest tone of disapproval is likely to elicit threats of moving out. Heaven help those incorrigible optimists who set out to spell some home truths to their progeny…all their years of sleepless nights and diapering and fretting will smoke out under the burning reminders of their parenting indiscretions. Do watch out for the pitch and tone in the voice, it can rake up their childhood traumas that plenty gets traced back to, in any case. The degree of parental expectations has steadily declined over the generations. It is cause for celebration and gratitude today if the offspring are happy, chilled out, and clear of trouble.

The kids did not ask to be born, remember!

Oh yes! Yes, yes, yes…I could have handled them with far greater sensitivity, for one. There is a list of attributes that

I now see I should have exhibited…greater humor for sure and some generic chill pill. My anticipatory antenna was too acutely humming and swinging in a constant effort to dodge the occasional gale. I might have worn a happier, more open expression, I don't know. I was too caught up trying to be a supportive, providing, inspiring, driving mother, walking a warpath towards a grand sum of opportunities for their growth.

Quite a self-deprecatory list there and some I can try and live with. What I see as my greatest failing as a mother is the fact that I did not have the courage and staying power to permit them their own mistakes.

There are schools of thought on this issue and I align with the one that says, the children must be given berth for the usual age-related foul-ups. It is a luxury I did not afford them. I read a whole lot of print on how kids must be left alone to gaze out the window and dream, taking in life's lessons at their own pace and sampling simple pleasures in an unhurried day but that did not happen. There was always a bus to catch, a test to prepare for, a performance to gear up towards, an essay to work on, and a trip to leave upon.

Right or wrong, I feared the uncertainty of uncertainty. I was afraid of the consequences of their unintentional mistakes. It is, of course, a whole lot easier today. They are self-driven, self-directed, and self-defined. It feels safe enough to let them be.

But if asked in retrospect, as to what might qualify as the greatest parenting skill, I would unhesitatingly and squarely put that as the "courage to let one's progeny make mistakes".

Good luck with that one though! You up to it? Better be.

The New Dad

My Dad, Col H S Sangha, is ahead of his times. Born in 1937, he often brews his own tea and tells his children that every person's health is their own responsibility. "The dissatisfaction some of my contemporaries expressed in their marital lives, I would tell them they should have gotten themselves a maid instead," he shares at times. His stories of riding to school astride a horse in Pakistan, the hockey-playing days in Ludhiana with his Punjab Agricultural College (now University) team, and going in search of his errant sibling around the by lanes of Moga, brandishing a hockey stick will live on in us. And there is a cue here for the modern dads.

My Dad swam against the stream, but you are the chosen one, sitting pretty on the most exciting time to be a father. There is an opportunity for you to parachute into the winds of sweeping change. You get to be soft as a pillow as well as tough as nails. There will be unfamiliar scenarios, new scripts, unknown turns, and a man's primal connection with his progeny.

There are two dynamics that have shifted recently to make all of this possible. A changing gender dynamic and the redefinition of masculinity. Moms have traditionally led the charge on housework and parenting, the appointment still holds. But more dads than ever before are attending parent-teacher meetings (PTMs), chauffeuring their children to classes, helping with the homework, and becoming at ease in the kitchen. And it does not stop at that. The emotional labour of being with your child through the fallout of heartbreak, disappointment, a poor test score, a threatening social media post or rejection from a friend is no longer just a mom's specialty. My husband is the go-to-parent for my girls quite often, for instance.

Along with this shift in gender dynamics, we are in the midst of dialogues about the definition and meaning of masculinity. Toxic masculinity has begun to be examined and derided. There is an acknowledgment of the sometimes invisible and unspoken negative effects it can wield, not just societally, but on women in particular.

It is such a leap from my grandfather who expressed his love by acquiring farming land and buying the family a white-coloured Ambassador MK III with the license plate PUK 1100. He barely spoke with his daughters, my aunts. The only physical display of affection was a quick and awkward, gaze averted, ruffle on the head! We graduated to a shoulder hug with my father from there. And today, it is perfectly permissible for fathers to bring their gentleness, their loving and demonstrative caring to this next generation. Not only do they get to model the strength that comes with kindness and vulnerability for their boys, they also get to guide their girls to look out for these qualities in their partners.

Truth be told, the argument back then that the division of labour made sense because it was the dads going out to work full time is falling through today when both parents are working and yet moms continue to carry the lion's share of parenting. There were and continue to be families where Dad is home all day with the kids. Some two decades ago, they left it all to their partners but mercifully, the new dads are doing more at home, including housework and parenting. They are far more engaged with the lives of their kids than any generation gone before. This counts for major progress in human civilization.

There are reasons and more for the voices of dads and men to be in the mix for the young right now. With women empowerment, the sexual revolution, #MeToo, and the LGBTQ activism and boys being spoken of as feeling adrift, there is no longer the luxury of turning a blind eye or covering the ears. Dads will have to enter the trenches with the moms; we literally need all hands-on deck. The young stand to benefit hugely from the full availability of another adult. There cannot be enough advocates for them as they negotiate the storms of adolescence which now extend well into young adulthood! The supportive voice of dad is crucial to not just families but society. Our young need to hear your thoughts on the changing tide. They need to see you treat Mom, and other women in your life, with respect, dignity, and equality. Let the children hear the contrast in your voice from Mom's, the two fall very differently.

Dads can add to the level of love and acceptance and comfort the young receive from family. The new generation is less at risk when their dads are more involved. There are definite signs of hope. It is not uncommon to see dads bringing their kids into medical sessions; many more are taking time out to attend psycho-education events. It is heartening to come across sites such as The New Dad—Home or The New Father: A Dad's Guide to the First Year or New Dad Survival Tips to Get You Through the First Month.

There are images online of awesome dads. A Dad who wore a skirt in solidarity with his dress-wearing son. There is one of the father who created beeping Easter eggs for his blind daughter to hunt. One dad went so far as to create educational pancakes for his kids. There is a father and his differently-abled son who compete together in various athletic events including marathons. Unbelievably, a dad dressed up as Red Riding Hood because his girl wanted to be the wolf.

This is the most important work guys could be doing in their lives but for this to happen, they need permission from their mothers, wives and society. They are missing out on all the good stuff that connection with the young is made up of. The young, in turn, stand to learn so much from the stories and experiences of their fathers.

Dads, your sagas will live on in your children. Parenting is difficult at times, but not much else you will ever do, be more enriching. Why would you ever give up your right to any of that?

The Vaping Point

Our kids are bored today like never before. And there are these demons dancing in their little minds. It is almost as though they have lost their sense of wonderment. We are too busy to look at them with light and love; we just want to get on with the business of them succeeding. In the absence of that all-important affirmative vibe at home and school, very often, they feel the need to 'feel' something, to try something new.

Concerns were raised in Rajya Sabha recently over children falling into the trap of drugs, with a Congress Member claiming that 25,000 school children in Delhi have turned addicts. In Punjab, an alarming 75% of its youth are said to be severely habituated. Mumbai, Hyderabad and other cities around the country are quickly clambering on to this train of grief. Distressingly so, the age of initiation gets younger and younger. A research published by the Indian Journal of Psychiatry, reveals that in India, by the time most children reach the ninth grade, about 50 percent have tried at least one of the illicit drugs.

However, this is not a time to be alarmed. Our young are as dismayed and confused when these substances appear in their young lives. What we can do is to listen to them from a position of knowledge.

So, to begin with, let's acknowledge that the taboo around drug use and abuse is losing ground fast. It was once considered the preserve of "naughty children" but that distinction is long gone.

Vaping and Juuling are the new gateway drugs used for coping and self-soothing. These are covert methods for ingesting nicotine and marijuana (pot/cannabis/weed/ganja/charas/bhang). Addiction can happen in a matter of weeks and young people are fascinated with the paraphernalia around it, the tanks, the mods, the Juul, the chargers, and the pods. Most of these devices fit neatly up one's sleeves or in a pocket of jeans or a backpack and because the output is vapor, it is either odorless or has a child-friendly smell like that of bubble gum or cereal.

Aside from vaping, Juuling, and marijuana the abuse of prescription drugs in India is gaining momentum. According to the United Nations Office on Drugs & Crime (UNODC) even though the law requires all drugs with "abuse potential" to be sold only on prescription, there is "significant diversion" from this. Sale of these lethal cocktails ranging from uppers to downers, benzodiazepines to hallucinogens is reflected in increased emergency room visits, overdose deaths, and treatment admissions for prescription drug use disorder. Teens themselves are also rather casual about dealing drugs. They will buy and sell for a select group of friends. And girls are now nearly as likely as boys to use regularly.

Today when a child mentions paper, do not jump to the conclusion that he is referring to chart paper! More and more young people take to weed, rolling joints that many parents and teachers cannot tell from regular cigarettes. There is an enticing cultural vibe around this substance moreover and plenty of fallacies of convenience. Children believe it is a plant, from the earth, far safer than alcohol because it does not tax a vital organ. The notion is that while weed smokers are recreational it is the alcohol drinkers that are hardcore.

But weed today is a deceptively dangerous substance. For one, it is the most demotivating drug out there associated with the erasure of memories and loss of life's essential spark. If the child is all of a sudden markedly lazy, elusive, the grades drop, he loses interest in the activities he once loved, if he changes friends, or if he starts to have trouble at school parents and teachers are to trust their instinct and ask the question. The tipping point happens when smoking weed shifts from being recreational to being medicinal. Young people begin to smoke not just to get high or stoned but to soothe anxiety, manage depression, numb feelings about falling grades or family or social issues. A lot of kids smoke at night to fall asleep. With no peace of mind, they try to medicate consciousness away, it is an effective escape from one's own psyche. The risk is in losing time and potential and connection with others. No longer just through bowls, joints, and bongs, weed can be vaped, Juuled, baked into brownies or edibles, distilled into wax like dabs and lollipops too.

Worryingly so, weed is a different drug altogether today, wildly more potent and addictive than before. Some of the most commonly used strains in use are as much as twenty or thirty times higher in THC (tetrahydrocannabinol, the mind-altering substance in weed) than the drug was thirty years back. Weed is unregulated since it is illegal still and it may come laced with some other drug like heroin, meth (methamphetamine), LSD (lysergic acid diethylamide/acid), or PCP (phencyclidine/angel dust). Weed is also notoriously easy to acquire today. Ask any square and scrubbed teenager and they will know dealer names, cell numbers, and houses. Its distribution channels are clean; you don't need to go heading into the dingy parts of cities, just regular spaces.

If your child is abusing drugs of any kind, the thing to do would be to first listen fully and completely without agenda and fear and judgment. Instead of focusing on the behaviour that seems unacceptable to us, therefore, focus on the why. Why do they use substances so frequently? What feelings does the drug protect them from? How else might they cope? Better be sincere and kind and have unconditional positive regard. Our children have ultra-sensitive detectors that ping at patronizing and vilifying and bullshitting. Kids are known to keep their consumption moderate when they can talk to their parents about it. A 'don't ask don't tell' policy would be as foolhardy a cat-and-mouse game as the 'search and destroy' theory in these circumstances. It might in fact be time to reach out to a therapist or addictions specialist for help.

Weed is nearing legalization and that will increase its usage and bolster the thinking that there is no downside, this is not true. Future red flags would look like a semester lost, friendships strained, and family relationships in turmoil.

Social inclusion, emotional resilience, and normative training would be the way to go. To resolve this humanitarian crisis, it might help to constantly remind ourselves that the opposite of addiction is connection.

The Mighty Parent

It is staring us in the face today, this alarming new frontier that our kids seem to face younger and younger. A quick search on the internet will throw up the disturbing new trend of self-harm and suicide among the young. According to the latest available data from the National Crime Records Bureau, a student commits suicide every hour in India. The world's second-most populous country of over 1 billion has one of the highest suicide rates among those aged 15 to 29.

The suicides begin in school; continue in college and into the late 20s. Academic stress, highly competitive admissions to prestigious institutions and the whimsical job market are all contributing factors. Add to this the fear of disappointing their ambitious parents and falling behind their peers. Ironically enough, even those students who eventually do pass the entrance exams feel even more pressure to excel at university, often taking their own lives when it all becomes too much.

What is going on here? Do we have an inkling of what it is like to be in the shoes our children wear today? For instance, do parents and teachers realize that suicidal thoughts are becoming increasingly ordinary and pedestrian among young people? Kids today talk with one another, rather freely, about their thoughts of hopelessness and self-harm ideation. At times there may be a vision of plans, they might even think of how people might react once they are gone?

What were we like in contrast? There was way lesser self-awareness, less insecurity, and fewer comparisons to others. Who cared at age eight or nine whether other kids were smarter, more athletic, better looking, and so on? There was protection from these painful comparisons and insecurities by way of distractions and buffers that cloaked us in a cottony cocoon.

Kids today are exposed to the stimuli that fuel these comparisons every single day. It is right there, in their pocket or close by, waiting to remind them of their "imperfections," real or merely perceived. Imagine this diminishing of their minds, bodies, and social capital entering the consciousness as constant flux, the terrifying notion that they are not good enough, that they may be unloved or worse, unlovable.

Dr. Harish Shetty, a psychiatrist at Dr. L. H. Hiranandani Hospital believes that an inability to cope with small frustrations, failure, and loss, often coupled with social alienation can prove critical for some students. Neerja Birla, the founder and chairperson of Mpower, a mental health organization, rightly points out that when it comes to mental health, Indian parents need to stop going into denial mode and issuing defensive statements like, "My child has no such problems!"

A survey by the Centre for the Study of Developing Societies reveals about 4 in 10 students in India have experienced bouts of depression in the last few years. Schools and colleges are inept at dealing with nervous breakdowns among students. They do not yet foster a culture of understanding and trust, empathy, and compassion.

As parents, therefore, we can no longer avoid the discussion of suicide and suicidal ideation with our children. There is more than one set of grieving parents out there who were wholly blindsided, unaware that suicide was even a thought in their child's mind. Most parents, quite understandably, will have fears that children will be suggestible, somehow, if we introduce the notion of suicide to them, that we might be planting the seed of an idea. Historically, there may have been a time when this was the case, and parents could protect children from that degree of hopelessness. Sadly, that time is quite long gone.

Knowing she has someone to talk with, someone who is open, non-judgmental, and not too afraid, is precisely what the teen suffering suicidal thoughts most needs. A safety plan can be enormously comforting too. No suicidal person truly wants to die. Most have been known to describe a "suicidal fog" in which all feels lost and hopeless. Providing them an option, a "call me without reservation," tends to allow for just enough hope to provide a beacon through the fog, one that can be truly lifesaving.

There is a new quasi-suicidal thinking afoot, the idea that "I am not going to do anything to hurt myself, but I don't care if I wake up tomorrow, either." We need to be alert, and ask "Does this have to do with the way you feel about yourself? The world? The future?" Consider too: Is your child quieter than she used to be? Is she spending more time alone? Is she down and sullen? Has her behaviour shifted dramatically? Does she suddenly seem buoyant and relieved after a period of depression? Any and all of these can be indications of suicidality, with many more precipitants, of course. That "suicide fog" can sweep over a child in the wake of a bad test score, or fear of a disciplinary issue, or the aftermath of a sudden breakup. So, ask if she is okay and be receptive to the answer, especially if it is a no.

The bottom line is this: we are losing far too many young people to suicide—bright, talented, beautiful young people who cannot see past the moment. We can no longer keep this issue under wraps, vaguely cloaked in shame. The world our children are growing up in is a far harsher place than the one we came of age in. The right thing to do therefore is to balance the harsh messages our children receive constantly with gentleness. They need to know, now more than ever, that they have a soft, available place to fall.

What will be your course of action therefore if your young one does happen to be suicidal? Should your child express that she is overtly suicidal in the moment that you ask, the immediate plan would be to call a suicide prevention helpline or get to one such centre should there be trouble connecting. This will ensure her safety right away and there will be professionals for guidance through the next steps. If your child expresses some degree of suicidal ideation, but she does not have a plan and clearly is no immediate threat to herself, the thing to do would be to seek a psychologist or licensed clinical social worker, with specific experience working with young people who have experienced this despair.

It is a mighty parent that has the presence of mind to use all of the tools at her disposal to help her child regain a sense of safety and well-being. Whatever it takes!

The Anxious Inheritors

All the smart marketing jargon, shrewd political negotiations, and original, earth-shaking ideas will come a cropper if we leave behind a world not fit enough for our young. The other worrying fact is that they themselves exhibit a troubling lack of resilience to make a go of the legacy they have received from us.

Do you remember how it was? There was a virtual cocoon of distance and silence around my generation as we advanced through our teen years into adulthood. There was space to breathe and hear ourselves think. There was only a trickle of information about our peers that reached us. We met them in school or college or at work and the rest of the time was spent at home, doing our own thing. The adult world inspired confidence and assurance.

The Zoomers today sit under a waterfall of information about everyone else their age across mother earth's curvature. There is no escaping how well or poorly they compare with their contemporaries. And it is not just them, their families know the degree of differences too because everybody is on the same social media platforms. There is no getting away.

Imagine going through life with gritted teeth, pictures of your batch mate's learning curve on LinkedIn, foreign exchange programs and that unholy trip to Netherland's 'Best Kept Secret' music festival competing with their Instagram retouched romance story. Everyone else appears to be sorted on all fronts, the cells on their life's Excel sheet tick marked, the columns under heads of family, work, love life, personal growth neatly summing up.

And there you are, at age 21, living in mortal fear of your house-of-cards falling. You know there is an unhinged white supremacist carrying the nuclear briefcase of the most powerful nation in the world. Your social media feed tells you about the glaciers sliding towards the plains. There are videos of plastic activists screaming at you that your body is spontaneously absorbing 5 gms of plastic every week. Your beau just cancelled on you. Your friends are telling you to jazz up your social life. Your parents observe that you do not have a community or tribe you belong to. Your grandmother has observations on your appearance. There seems no respite.

These are heart-breaking times. Youth was supposed to be the spring of life, a time of promise and vitality looking ahead with eyes of wonder. Instead, you have Zoomers aged 14 on medication protocol for anxiety. Those young bodies have already seen enough. These are spirits that are perplexed at the chaotic waves of misinformation, polarizing views, and poorly researched opinions crashing against their weary minds. It is not unusual to have a Zoomer share, "There is nothing to look forward to." And this if you are honoured enough to be privy to the workings of their inner minds. For the rest of us, it is withdrawal, disconnect, even dissonance. Families are no longer able to keep up with their young, that space has been taken over by friends, therapists, YouTube, and Google.

My generation and Gen X frequently wonder what the fuss is all about. Did we not provide well enough for our Millennials and Zoomers? Have we not been in standby mode for them since forever? Do we not keep them fed, hydrated, and financed enough? When did we not drop everything to rush to assist them in their hour of crisis? Is it not abundantly clear that we stay informed of their whereabouts and keep track of their life events? What more could we be doing?

Ironically enough, this defensive self-dialogue reaches the Zoomers only to add to their anxiety.

It might stun older generations to know that the Zoomers, many of them are anxious at an existential level, wondering about the meaning of life. There is a never before ambivalence about the significance of their own living. Of course, there is anxiety about money, will there be enough of it? There is a latent resentment at the climate change, the quality of political discourse, the state of security in public spaces, the sudden jolt of their phone buzzing, a school/work alert or update. The anxiety looms, like a dark cloud overhead; coupled with a keenly felt awareness of not just the passage of time but also the scope of a lifetime that they fail to make sense of without panic flooding their young minds.

The troubling fact is that this anxiousness stemming from their hyper-competitive lives infests the entire gamut, right from the honour student to the home-work avoidant quarter. Both struggle with the moment-to-moment, day-to-day stress in their lives, the first by seeking therapy and the second by going into hiding and self-medicating with drugs, alcohol, video-games, or binge-watching. Few and fortunate are the Zoomers who are able to go unscathed by anxiety today.

Anxiety can hit as dizziness, nausea, headache, or even joint pain. A panic attack may appear in the form of symptoms reflecting an excruciating fear. Most people, if pushed will probably admit to an ongoing state of anxiety, a persistent buzz of dread at the back of their minds. It can take many forms. Zoomers may likely respond by avoiding school. Some may blank out during tests or public speaking. For others, anxiety can cause acid reflux. It is common to experience an impulse to vape or grab the phone or just act out. The heart can knock and the blood pressures shoot up. The manifestations of profound anxiety are all around us.

In order to understand how pervasive and intrusive this phenomenon is, I would urge you to watch *Angst*, an IndieFlix Original Documentary designed to raise awareness around anxiety. The film includes interviews with kids, teens, educators, experts, parents, and a very special interview with Michael Phelps. The goal of the film is to help people identify and understand the symptoms of anxiety and encourage them to reach out for help. The film screening also provides tools, resources, and above all, hope.

Just below that surface of anxiety and self-loathing borne by many Zoomers, there is a special courage, and strength and kindness. I can't think of a bigger mandate than to help them see these qualities in themselves without a crisis precipitating their awareness.

The message that needs to go to our Zoomers is that balance and goodness of fit at work and emotional wellness are in the final analysis, the cornerstones of success.

The Kinder Shopper

In 1998, my husband and I visited Kansas City to attend our niece's wedding. We carried the traditional, crimson red wedding "*lehenga*" for the bride. It had been painstakingly made by hand in an extended family boutique. The weight and volume really tested us on the international flight.

A few years later, it was the bride's sister, our other niece announcing her marriage. "What will the colour be this time?" I remember thinking. Imagine my surprise when I learnt she was going to use her sister's wedding dress, thank you. Her decision made a somewhat vague sense to me back then, it makes perfect sense today. She was a Zoomer before her time!

A big shift is happening in the world of buying and selling. Did you think for instance that it is just the Indians sweating a bargain? Price has begun to excite the Zoomer as much; in fact it is emerging as their primary motivator when shopping. And this is not for lack of money, their Gen X parents provide well and many have their personal sources of income.

And the difference does not stop at just the price but in the entire shopping experience. Going to a physical store to try out clothes is becoming rarer, the Zoomer shops mostly online. And if they don't like what arrives, well, they can always sell it back online!

This is the new wave of consumers a brand's online selling strategy has to serve. The problem is, these shoppers between the ages of 13 and 21, who are gearing up to enter the workforce find it impossible to be loyal to a brand. What could be the reasons for this fickleness? One, the brands are too expensive and two, the Zoomers come armed with their smartphones, they have the agile ability to instantly verify anything online.

I see it in my own family. It is hard to get our family Zoomers to match the enthusiasm of their grandmother for an expensive jaunt to the 17 Sector in Chandigarh. The young meander around listlessly while my mother tires out slowly, fighting to keep a cheerful face through the obvious indifference her precious grandchildren show to the big brands all around them. I remember being miffed at her disappointment until a friend sent me the WhatsApp promo of "Mumbai's first curated exhibit of Indian Upcycling designers." It read like the epitaph of the big guns in the apparel market. The brands featuring at this event had names like 'We are labeless' and 'Slow' and 'LataSita' and 'Swavlambi'.

Amrita Neelakantan, a speaker and thought leader at the event, conservation scientist with a Ph.D. from Columbia University, now teaching at the NIFT Delhi, spoke of her venture "Black Orchid". The new fashion initiative suggested a different perspective on clothing. Their essential idea was SURE - Sustainably Use Reduce Exchange ecosystem for clothing. You could buy a dress, wear it, swap with other items for only postage and a nominal cleaning fee. Perfect ecological, social and financial sense, the Zoomer way.

It stands to reason that unconventional forms of shopping such as these involving rental and resale would serve a generation that frequently documents their life on social media and is forever under pressure for new clothes. The idea after all is to stand out without spending an unholy amount of money. Gen Z is thrifty above all. Fiscally practical, they will not want to pay full price for anything; what drives them is value. And the alternative to getting this at a low price is to invest in more expensive things with longer lives.

Whatever the choice, being broke is one thing Zoomers cannot stand, and rightfully so, considering they would have been about 7 years young during the global financial downturn of 2008. Their spending habits were likely passed down by their parents and teachers, who were themselves shaped by the recession.

Speaking value, brands are quite obviously beginning to work extra hard to earn the Zoomer's trust. Transparency and authenticity are important to the Zoomers, more than ever before and more than to anyone else. The questions out there are: Does your brand have an unlimited returns policy on unworn items? Do you offer a repair service for worn clothing? Are you a tiny store that not many come to? Do you allow consumers to rent up to three items at any given time for a monthly fee? Are you able to be real and laugh at yourself? Are you using memes to market your offerings?

This is a highly informed cohort we are talking about. They will want to take charge of their lives and their futures. They have grown up around enough threats and uncertainty to leave the locus of control any place else. We are all moving into the unfamiliar territory of no-photo-retouching, undoctored images, real models. And there is still no guarantee however that the Zoomers will stick around even after a brand has aligned with their values of inclusivity, diversity, and youth empowerment. If you are slow to engage or you break your promise, the Zoomers will zip past in less than the blink of an eye.

Those times of being defined by your brands are long gone. The Zoomers are creating their own personal brands. A brand today is something that is perceived and marketed by the influencer who wears it. I recently attended a webinar on "The importance of early styling to enhance your child's individuality". My initial reaction was of alarm at what I read as an added pressure on the Zoomers but it is beginning to make sense now. After all, the Zoomers do live lives in pictures and do value standing apart.

So how does this most photographed generation strike a balance between their sustainability goals and their need for newness? The answer brings us back to the ideas of rental, resale and thrift. Slow fashion as against fast fashion that contributes to criminal waste. Thoughtful shopping makes it possible for Zoomers to flip their wardrobe without hurting the environment.

Here is a generation that lives in the cloud, uses thrift to create their own story and accepts diversity like no other group in the past. When you are so focused on including every shade, how could you yourself not stand out?